# Advance Praise for
## *Invisible Courage*

"If I could choose one book for seeking an authentic life - *Invisible Courage* would be it. Powerful, daring, honest, true, and to the point. Its message will speak to your heart in a way that is moving. An extraordinary book from an extraordinary, daring, and loving woman."
— Linda Pestana, Author of *Voices of the Heart*

"Filomena Tripp's *Invisible Courage* is an amazing account of a life lived to inspire. We are all connected; we all have infinite value, and *Invisible Courage* is a well-written reminder of how the human spirit is the strongest force in the universe. I highly recommend it!"
—Steve Manchester, #1 Bestselling Author of *The Rockin' Chair* and *Ashes*

"Filomena Tripp's *Invisible Courage* is a journey into Filomena's soul as well as our own. Through adversity with derogatory looks and words; she came to realize none of it represented the truth of who she is. Filomena is love in motion. She has realized her gift in speaking to all ages, instilling in every person that each of them have value. She has found love in her relationships and with her Higher Source, reaching a place of loving herself in all her glory exactly as she is… in perfect form."
—Deborah Beauvais, Owner of Dreamvisions 7 P    Network

D11153552

"Adequate social integration for people with disabilities; this has been a life long goal of Filomena Tripp. Her book Invisible Courage tracks that journey beginning with her personal struggles, followed by the plight of the disabled community. This book is a must read for anyone interested in compassion and courage."

—Roberto Medeiros, Camara Municipal da Lagoa,
Vereador Vice-Presidente, 1990 a 2009

*Dear Patrons,*

# Invisible Courage

*May you find inspriation
from my experiences.*

*Thank you*

*Filomena Tripp*

## by Filomena Tripp

### with Janine Ouellette Sullivan

Published in the United States of America

ISBN 978-1-5323-5170-9

Cover and interior design by Kaitlin Sullivan

Published 2017

# Contents

# Preface

by Janine Ouellette Sullivan

THE STORY TOLD IN THIS book is both revealing and intriguing. Rarely do we have an opportunity to get to know a person in a way that is conveyed with such gentle power. Filomena Tripp, born with such severe physical deformities that experts believed she would not live more than twenty- four hours, had been met with one defeat after another. Her life was truly the stuff of which nightmares are made. Through it all, there was always a part of her that knew her life was worth living.

From her humble childhood home in São Miguel, Azores to a thriving productive life in New Bedford, Massachusetts, Filomena determined that nothing she set her mind to was impossible. I witnessed her compassion for people and the gentle courage that blossomed from her ability to love herself. A dynamo, an activist for people with no voice, this woman is changing lives with one action after another. She reveals, in *Invisible Courage,* that her personal truth is what matters. She refused to believe negative expectations put upon her because of her birth defects; this belief was sincerely an act of insight and faith.

I believe Filomena's life and the message she delivers with *Invisible Courage* are meant to set an example to show us all that we should accept who we are, love who we are, and live the best life possible. She is the personification of fearlessness and a testimony to the need for us all to respect life. *Invisible Courage* proves that we all matter; we all have purpose and value.

# Acknowledgments

WHILE WRITING *INVISIBLE COURAGE,* I learned a great deal about myself and the people in my life. Words alone cannot express how blessed I have been throughout my life.

I give thanks to God who has loved me each and every day. I could do nothing without God's undying love and compassion.

To my husband, Jim, my best friend and confidant. Jim has loved me unconditionally and supported all my dreams—even the wild ones. His love lifts my spirit and gives me wings to fly. He is a gift and a blessing to me.

To my loving family, my first husband Luis, and friends who stood with me throughout my journey. Without your love and support, I would not be the person I am today.

To Roberto Medeiros, whom I met many years ago. He knew I had an important story to share; his encouragement and support motivated me to tell my story. He gave me my first opportunity to speak before a large crowd. I was invited there to encourage people to do their best in life. It was then that I realized I had a calling to share my story.

I am grateful to my friend Janine Ouellette Sullivan who heard my story told from the depth of my heart. She believed this was an important story to share with people everywhere; she was instrumental in helping me realize the dream of publishing this memoir.

I have met great people who, in one way or another, have guided me on my journey. It is impossible to name everyone, but know that you are in my prayers and I am grateful for each of you.

Each moment of my life has molded me into the person I have become. God has blessed me greatly.

# To My Dear Readers

SHARING MY STORY HAS BEEN one of the hardest things I have ever done. Revisiting difficult situations and acknowledging very unsettling emotions has had me in tears on several occasions. Exposing my life and bearing my soul has been a true leap of faith. I needed to trust that my story was valuable and worthy of being shared. I needed to abandon my shame. I needed to accept that my path was, and continues to be, paved with blessings.

My intention in writing this book is to inspire people with disabilities. As I proceeded to get my thoughts onto paper, I realized my intention grew to include anyone who wished to live the best life possible with whatever he/she had to contend with.

I hope and pray that my readers will look deeply into their lives, seek devoutly, and realize they are important. All lives have value.

I want you to deeply understand that you are beautiful just as you are. I encourage you to free yourself from anger, shame, and fear. Live to the fullest the life you have been given. Be the gift you were created to be and remember, loving yourself is the first step. Your corner of the world needs the very best of what you have to offer.

God bless you,

Filomena

# Dedication

I DEDICATE *INVISIBLE COURAGE* TO my husband, Jim.

Having someone who loves me unconditionally has been one of the greatest gifts I have received. And although I have missing body parts, Jim sees me as the whole person I am. He knows my heart and soul, and he has nurtured me more than I could have ever imagined.

When I think, "Jim really loves me," my heart fills with a sense of endless possibilities.

Being loved so purely by my husband has truly given me wings to fly.

Jim is an example of what God calls us to be to one another: loving, kind, and gentle. Together, we have brought out the best in one another; that is what love does. We have grown in a marriage that deepens in love as each new day begins. His love and encouragement makes visible what was once invisible within.

Together, we are living a dynamic life, full of joy and purpose. I am extremely grateful for my husband's total support.

To Jim—I love you with all my heart.

# Introduction:
# The Storm

*"Start where you are.*
*Use what you have.*
*Do what you can."*

—*Arthur Ashe*

RAIN POUNDED AGAINST THE WINDOWS of my small apartment in South Dartmouth, Massachusetts. Each noisy raindrop clambered against the window pane, scraping against my unsettled soul.

Tears ran down my cheeks on an even pace with the raindrops. Thunder rang in the distance and echoed the agony that was no match for the storm within my soul. As I reached toward the ceiling with my half arms, I was certain that serenity existed only in a remote part of the world— certainly not in mine. "I cannot do this!" I bowed my head and caught a barrage of tears on the stumps of both arms. Over and over, I whimpered and chanted. "I cannot do this any longer! I cannot do this any longer!" This was a feeble attempt to convince myself that I would not yield to defeat. But my life was not listening, or so it seemed.

This crossroad, this seemingly unalterable destiny, would spin my life in a new pain- filled direction. Unbeknownst to me, on this heart-breaking day, I had not yet reached my lowest point or met my deepest sorrow. Three long years of sheer agony was yet to come. At the age of thirty-four, broken by more than three decades of struggle to prove that I was capable of a normal life, I, Filomena Tripp, fell into the abyss of deep depression.

# Chapter 1:
# The Struggle Begins

*"Let no one disqualify you."*

—*Colossians 3:18*

I THOUGHT THAT MAYBE I was never meant to live a relatively normal life. Perhaps everything I had been told from childhood was true. Maybe every part of my body, inside and out, was a mess, waiting to fail in one way or another. The declarations spoken by so many assured me that I had not been meant to live. The memory of those words pierced my heart like a lightning bolt, sending shock waves through my body.

I was born on October 8, 1955 in Santa Cruz, Villa de Lagoa, São Miguel, Azores, one of nine volcanic islands in the North Atlantic Ocean, west of Portugal. I was the addition to a family of two girls and three boys, along with my mother and father. Prior to my birth, my mother lost a set of twins due to a drastic medical situation. Eventually, two more children would arrive to round out a family of ten. Times were challenging. Our home was simple and functional. We raised chickens for eggs and meat; we raised pigs to add to our food supply, as well. Our garden provided vegetables. We did not have much, but we always had food on the table. My mother baked the most delicious bread in our wood-fed oven, and a large pot of soup filled with chicken and garden vegetables would sit and simmer on top of the stove. Our neighbors lived similar lives. People did not have much money. Instead, we learned to make the best of what we had, to stretch it out, and to make even a bowl of soup and a slice of freshly baked bread a memorable meal.

Before I was born, news of deformed babies had sent shock through our village. Hysteria swirled; tales of babies born with the head of a horse or the face of a dog circulated. The freakish descriptions grew more gruesome, as the stories were relayed from person-to-person. It was as though a curse had befallen the island, and pregnant women continuously prayed that their babies would be spared.

But my mother was not spared. Upon my birth, the obstetrician approached her to inform her that her baby girl was born with many abnormalities. He explained that I had been born with no lower arms and, therefore, no hands, and that only one of my legs had developed. He further revealed that my internal organs were likely deformed as well, although he did not know for certain. Since my mother had not taken any medications known to cause birth defects, it was a mystery, never to reveal what had caused my birth defects. Anguish consumed my mother, as the doctor went on to say that he did not think that I would live more than twenty four hours. He advised her to quickly baptize and name me before I died.

My mother later told me that between her tears and sorrow, she offered prayers on my behalf. And twenty four hours later, I was still alive. I began my life by beating the odds, much to the surprise of the medical staff. However, soon after, the doctor revisited my mother. He now rationalized that there was no hope for me to live a normal life. Therefore, he recommended that if I was to continue to beat the odds and live another day, that she should authorize them to give me an injection that would end my life. Basically, they asked my mother to euthanize me to save the family from the torture that he thought I would bring upon them.

I was told that at this suggestion, my mother cried out in fear and confusion, uncertain of what she should do. She already had several children at home for which she had to care and the revelation of my very poor prognosis caused her further anguish. Again, the doctor advised her to end my life. Years later, Momma told me that at that moment God spoke to her heart. She felt a silent and calming feeling, as though God was standing at her side and guiding her through this difficult time. As a result of His message, she wrapped me in a blanket, cradled me in her arms, and prepared to take me home. If my mother had listened to her doctor, I would not be alive today. I am very thankful that she made the choice she did; it just took me a while to realize it.

As a general rule, people accept doctor's advice quite readily. Regardless of the cause, I was born with extensive birth defects; my family thought that, for sure, I would not survive long past my toddler years. Some people in our small village actually thought I *should* die. My abnormalities frightened them; unfortunately, fear creates unsound thinking in many people. As it turned out, in every other way I was a healthy child. Apart from undeveloped limbs, my physiology was as healthy as my mind. But I did not learn that concept until I was well into adulthood. Instead, I grew up believing that I was deformed—both inside and out.

*Baby Filomena*

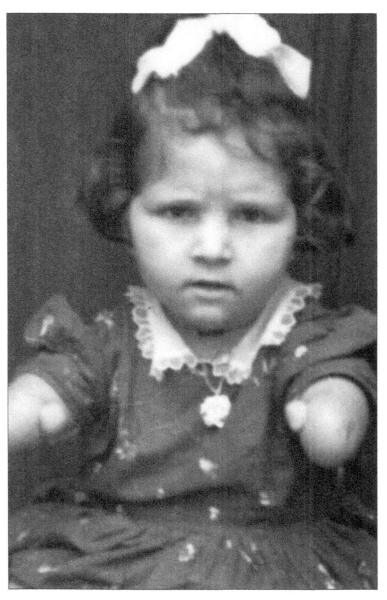

*Filomena at age 1*

# Chapter 2:
# My Early Years

*"I don't care what the stars say about how
small we are. One, even the smallest, weakest,
most insignificant one, matters."*

—Rick Yancey, *The 5th Wave*

As a toddler, I figured out how to get myself around.
Children are very adaptive in that way. I used to wiggle and
shuffle along the floor or yard on my buttocks, so I could get
where I wanted to go; this gave me a sense of independence. I
did not have to rely on someone to carry me around or push
me in a wagon or carriage. Down ten steps or so from our back
patio was the chicken coup and the pig pen. I used to wiggle
down those steps on my behind, moving my hips from side-to-
side like a penguin to get to the pen area where I watched the
animals. I didn't care for the chickens and pigs very much, but
they did entertain me. They were noisy and smelly; the noisy
grunts reminded me of the whispers people thought I could
not hear. I wanted to let them out of their pens; I imagined

they could stand up on their hind legs and reach with their front legs to open the gate. After all, I had many six-legged ant friends that were free to move about wherever they liked. *But since pigs had only four legs and chickens, two, then perhaps freedom was measured in the quantity of limbs?* That was the reasoning of a child with missing limbs.

The ants—my quiet, soothing friends. While my mother would wash clothes on the patio using a cement basin and hand-crafted pins, I would entertain myself. By digging into the brick wall with the big toe of my right foot, I was free for a while. I focused only on the bricks, dusty cement, and what lived inside the wall. I had seen the ants many times in the past and I was trying to find their nest. There was something entertaining and relaxing about this activity as living, moving creatures intrigued me. The ants were passive, pleasant bugs, unassuming and free to roam. I was also fascinated by the cooperation the ants had with one another. *Where are the ants going? What are they doing? How do they manage to live so well together?* Back and forth, dozens of the tiny black creatures moved along the patio to the wall. Each had a job and a purpose. Fascinated, day-after-day, I played with the insects. Meanwhile, I heard the echoed voices of adults who looked on, saying, "Oh, the poor crippled child."

Only the objective eye of an innocent child could find the hidden mystery behind a colony of ants. Curious by their co-operative movements, I did not yet have the ability to articulate my imperative question: *Why do the ants co-exist in what looks like a harmonious environment?* Eventually, I would notice

8

the differences between acceptance and cooperation at the human level versus my friends, the ants. But back then, ants were my escape from reality and a doorway to a dream that relieved what I felt, which as early as the age of four, was a bleak existence. Under the summer sky, watching an ant colony build a cooperative society was where I found peace. Little did I know that those ants would have a tremendous impact on my life.

As a child, I wanted the same things that other children wished for. I wanted to play outside, kick up dirt in the street, hop in puddles after the rain, dance, learn at school, and make friends. I desired to laugh, scrape my knees, and have a crush on a boy at school. My missing arms and leg did not impede my desire to be like the other children or to interact with them.

However, I was not able to do such things. My parents' belief in my limitations, mixed with their desire to shield me from ridicule, laced my lonely days.

My horizons widened a bit more when my aunt, living in America, sent me a manual push wheelchair, as there were none in our village at that time. I acquired the freedom gained from mobility; it was difficult, but I felt liberated. The more I was able to transport myself around, the less humiliating my movements felt, especially as I got older. Still, my family thought it would be best to shelter me from what could be a cruel environment. It was not by unkind intent that they kept me from mainstream life; it was simply to protect me from more hurt and pain. Regardless, the taunting came.

I remember when I was six years old or so, I was lifted into a chair by the window. Someone thought it would be pleasing for me to look out at other children as they played. I looked out at them running and jumping along the unpaved street; they kicked up dust, while singing and skipping about. They filled the air with laughter and song. It was so painful watching this joyous activity. But outside, the children would call me names like "crippled" and worse.

They spoke to me in a way that told me, as young as I was, that I was not welcome to join in their playtime. *Even the chickens in the back yard can roam free*, I thought to myself. As a result, most times, I only looked on.

What many people did not understand was that my heart was born full of curiosity just like any other child's. My mind was perfectly normal; it was my body that was altered by some kind of genetic glitch. I longed for the things the children in my village took for granted. I was so confused. Looking through that window, I wondered, W*hy am I this way? Where do I fit in?* My heart broke time and time again.

I couldn't help but notice that people turned away when they saw me, while countless nasty comments came my way. I was an angry, bold child because of the cruelty and the commentary to which I was constantly exposed. Yet I understood that if I accepted these actions as "normal," I would surely die inside. That word "normal" was a curiosity to me. *What, exactly, is normal? Should I accept the cruelty and the defeatist attitude as the normal way to live my life?* I hoped not, but people did look at me like I was less than human, like I was an underachiever of "normal." I could think, talk, and feel just like everyone else. *Therefore, I AM a NORMAL girl who was born into a body that is NOT.* I knew such deep sorrow at such a young age because I could not seem to find a way to fit in and have people accept me for *me.* My thoughts constantly searched for doorways to possibilities, but my body was an obstacle to overcome. I knew I had to fight to figure out what life in my body would mean for me. That took a great deal of time.

*Filomena at age 3*

*From Left to Right: Valdemira (sister), Adelino (father), Adelino (brother), Maria Estrela (mother), Filomena, Jose (brother), Joao (brother), and Maria Eduarda (sister)*

# Chapter 3:
# Smile Though Your Heart Is Breaking

*"When you focus on being blessed, God makes sure that you are always blessed in abundance."*

—*Joel Osteen*

MY PRIMARY GOAL WAS TO be like other people so I could fit in. That seemed like a good first step. Early on, I would watch my cousin, Deolinda, eat food and hold utensils in her hands. She helped teach me how to eat properly. Mostly through observation, I learned to hold a fork, a knife, and a spoon, using my stump arms and my knob of a thumb. After a great deal of practice, I was able to eat food without leaning into my bowl to get it. In addition, this allowed me to avoid getting food all over my face and clothing. This was a big step toward social acceptance.

I taught myself how to accomplish feats just by watching. My eyes were fixed on simple things like turning a page in a book, reaching for a cup in the kitchen, turning a handle on a door, and switching on a light. Paying attention to acts as simple as pouring a glass of juice from a bottle required me to have the insight to plan each movement ahead of time. Every observation was an opportunity to learn. Every struggle to learn was a move toward independence. And every step toward independence gave me confidence.

Tina, my sister, helped me as well. Even though she was several years younger than I, she was like a mother to me. She was someone with whom I could talk about anything, and I could divulge my feelings to her. She was not judgmental; she loved me and wanted to be helpful. Both she and my friend, Luisa, were my lifelines during my childhood years of great isolation. They treated me like a human being, not a cripple or a non-human. They gave me my greatest gift— happy childhood memories. We would play house, dress up our dolls, and make up stories of the future. Our playtime was lighthearted and joyful. The compassion these girls offered me in an otherwise sheltered world provided me with a semblance of a normal childhood. These friendships would be an experience that would solidify the hopeful foundation on which I could build a positive life, a life I wished to live well.

We were innocent children who played with and spent time with each other. The love we shared blessed the experience of learning new and useful skills. As I received this nurturing, I felt less and less like a human castaway. Thus, my "normalcy" at this point helped me to thrive and I started realizing that I could begin carving out a niche in my life.

But sometimes, every step forward is countered with one step back. Don't misunderstand.

I found happiness in bits and pieces in my life. I was an adventurous child who had a grand imagination. I had many loving people in my life who cared about me. So I learned, at a young age, to put a fake smile on my face. I thought that was a good start to self-acceptance and acceptance from others. I mean, a smile is a welcoming action, right? If only something so simple could be a real solution.

# Chapter 4:
# Peddled Through
# the Village

*"Sometimes it's not enough to know
what things mean, sometimes you have
to know what things don't mean."*

—*Bob Dylan*

From the time that I could remember until the time I was ten, my father, in an effort to gain sympathy and monetary donations, would take me around the island on weekends, especially if there was a feast or any type of public gathering. He actually exhibited me throughout surrounding towns and villages. This mercenary claimed that our family needed money for my care. People would feel sorry for me and give him money. Pictures of me were sent to America so that family members would pity me and donate to his cause. Unfortunately, a good deal of the money collected went to my father and little to my care.

I remember one especially horrid occasion that caused me great suffering. To add to the collection for my "care," my father took me to a larger city, Ponta Delgada. A man, dressed in nice clothing, approached. My father, thinking that the man had money, approached him and asked him to donate to my support. This nicely dressed man was actually an undercover policeman. Even at ten years old, I understood the conversation going on between them as the officer proceeded to escort us, presumably to the police station. I was so scared that I suddenly took sick to my stomach, and I, in my terror, actually wet my pants. Fortunately, instead of the police station, the officer brought us to the bus stop and told my father that he should never return to the city again. This was one of the worst experiences of my young life. It both scared me and scarred me. To this day, I still get nervous when I see a police officer. Being put on display like a freak in a traveling circus was beyond humiliating. I became very hateful toward my father. I'd think, *How can he take advantage of me this way?* I also became distrustful of people's intentions after this humiliating experience. *How and where can I escape this painful degradation?*

My mother and siblings hated that my father would embarrass and humiliate me by taking me to solicit donations. They knew that his actions were wrong, but they felt helpless. They sensed he was destroying my spirit, but they were afraid of him. My father was of the "old school" and known to be stern and inflexible. He ruled with the expectation that no one would dare question him or confront him. They didn't, and I didn't either. But I lost out on yet another one of my freedoms because I refused to continue to be his part-time job. Because I refused to let my father parade me around to elicit pity and monetary gain, he refused to let me go to church.

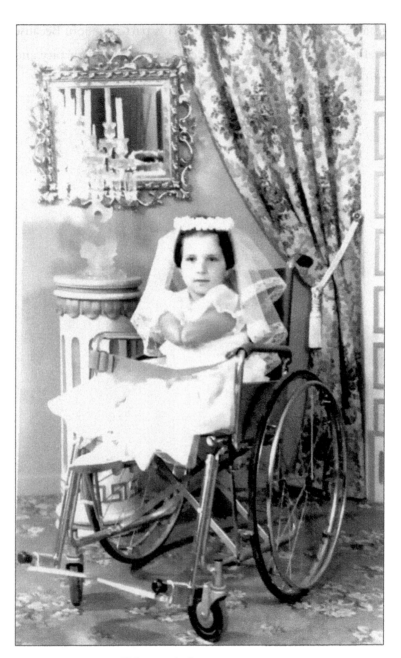

*Filomena's first communion*

# Chapter 5:
# Nurturing Inner Guidance

*"Making a dream into reality begins with what you
have, not with what you are waiting on."*

—*T. F. Hodge*

Although my family was not particularly religious, I loved
attending mass; I longed to be at church and learn about the
kind of peace that God could offer me. I held, as strongly as a
child could, to the belief that God was good, kind, and loving.
Fortunately, before my father banned me from church, I had
received catechism study. My catechism book was a wonderful tool to strengthen my belief in God. My catechism studies
showed other children that I had more in common with them
than they might have thought. Slowly but surely, I began to fit
in with these other children; I was overjoyed to be included in
their activities and programs. My loneliness was softened by
these accomplishments and social interactions. Finally, I progressed through catechism and enjoyed receiving the holy sac-
rament of Reconciliation, and I made my First Communion

at Ingreja de Santa Cruz Church. But because I was still quite young, my idealism often clashed with reality.

I was taught to believe, and indeed I did believe, that God is love. Yet people continued to be unkind to me. When I was hurting, I would ask God, *Why is this happening to me? My siblings were healthy. What happened to me and my life?* It seemed like Rejection and Ridicule were scabs that were too often picked at. I tried to reconcile the different behaviors and reactions that I was exposed to. I knew that God loved me. I just didn't understand how He was supposed to show that love to me. *Look at the body He has given me!* So I continued to cling to the belief that His unconditional love for me would help me to understand. And I valued the few people who accepted me as I was; they took the time to see past the missing limbs. They were the real treasures in my life. But like children do, I wavered back and forth between whatever happiness I could find in my life and the pain of living it.

At that time, I could understand God's love for me. But trying to connect to my peers and other members of society was a bit more difficult. Maybe it was a lack of understanding or the fact that people were not used to seeing someone with my level of disability. Glares and negative comments from others were part of my daily ordeal. I learned early on that people feared what they did not understand; perhaps, without realizing it, they then responded in negative ways. I made a simple connection in my young mind: *If a person feels fear, for example, of an insect, the immediate reaction is to kill it.* And many times, I felt like that bug. But what could I possibly do that could be so harmful to anyone? All I wanted was to be accepted, to be "normal." That might have been one of the reasons why I enjoyed playing with the ants so much during my childhood. The ants did not fear me; they were also protected within the wall from those who would stomp on them or kill them. I sensed that the wall that protected the ants was no different from the wall of fear that people built to separate themselves from those who differ from them. *Do they realize that their wall of "protection" from the disabled becomes my wall of isolation?* Brick-by-brick, the wall grew taller, starting at my birth. I longed to dismantle that wall. At an early age, I realized that part of my future was going to involve helping people to overcome their fears.

However, there were many years of struggle ahead, and I did not realize that I would have to overcome my own fears and feelings of inadequacy before I was in the position to help others in any meaningful way.

# Chapter 6:
# My Soul, My Body, Now My Mind

*"I think the girl who is able to earn her own living and pay her own way should be as happy as anybody on earth. The sense of independence and security is very sweet."*

—*Susan B. Anthony*

ATTENDING SCHOOL IN A REGULAR classroom was out of the question. My family wanted to protect me from failure and rejection. Schools in São Miguel were not equipped for children with any type of disability. The truth was, the school would not allow me to attend. Those in charge thought I might be hurt by the other children, who would say thoughtless and unkind words to me.

Ironically, the adults making that decision only perpetuated the ostracism; by keeping me away, the children remained unfamiliar with those different from themselves, thereby inviting even more unkind words for the disabled.

My father hired a tutor for me when I was eight years old. I would wiggle my little bottom wherever I needed to go to meet with her. Although I had the wheelchair that my aunt had sent, I did not want to rely on anyone to push me to my tutoring appointments. I was continually working toward independence; I knew that education was a major step in that direction. I was very eager to learn new things and keep pace with the other children. In my mind, wobbling down the sidewalk to the tutor proved to all who looked on just how determined I was to be educated. I knew that education was my passport to freedom in a world that offered me one road block after another.

I met with my tutor five times a week. Every day, I would work my lessons in Portuguese. Afterward, I would practice what I had learned. I knew it was only a matter of time before I learned to write, spell, and understand mathematics. Learning was a way for me to show people that I was a thinking, reasoning person. Getting an education caused me to think about my future and my place in the world. This was an exciting time for me, as I met each challenge with unflinching devotion and desire to overcome each stumbling block. The smile I had on my face reassured people that I was doing what was best for my future, and it showed that I was proactive in my personal wellbeing. That smile, however, hid fear, anger, and insecurity. But I would not allow that to stop me. Failure to progress would mean my life was doomed. Those thoughts never felt like an exaggeration to me. I had to keep pace, or my future would be limited.

The everyday actions a child my age took for granted were monumental challenges for me. I learned to read and write when I was older than most children. I had to learn how to hold a pen and to write using no hands. With a pencil secured between the rounds of my stump arms, I guided it through the motions using slight pressure from my mouth. What might have seemed like an ordinary task to others was an extraordinary one to me at the age of eight. It was a euphoric feeling, at age ten, to write my name for the first time. Filomena. I thought, *Yes! Me! A person that matters!* Filomena Melo. *I am Filomena Melo, and I am a valuable person in this life.* Filomena Melo, *That's me!* This felt wonderful. It was much the way a young person might act when he or she has a crush on someone; the name of the crush is written over and over again. I admired my signature. This achievement allowed me the biggest and brightest smile. Oddly enough, writing my name opened a window for me to see myself more clearly, to be more self- reliant and independent. Or maybe it was that I could accomplish a feat that most "normal" people could. Writing my name was like making a contract with myself to keep moving forward with my accomplishments and show people that I could be a person too, regardless of my missing extremities.

# Chapter 7:
# Moving to America

*"One is never afraid of the unknown; one is afraid
of the known coming to an end."*

—*Jiddu Krishnamurti*

WHILE I WAS GROWING UP in São Miguel during the 1950s
and 60s, there was very little support available for the disabled.
Services and equipment for people with special needs came
much later. Society did not welcome people with disabilities;
this segment of the population was often kept out of sight.
Public buildings, such as schools, were not accessible or welcoming to those who would require extra help or attention.
There were no wheelchairs, let alone ramps to enable their use.
For the most part, I found the doors to normal life closed to
people with any sort of physical or mental disability. This was
not a negative view on my part; this was the reality for people
with disabilities at this time. Life was already a struggle; added
difficulties of mobility and social acceptance made the experience worse. But I was one of the lucky ones who stayed at

home with my family where I was being loved. Many unfortunate people suffered under miserable conditions, isolated in institutions.

As I grew older, my challenges grew larger; the concerns of a child are not the same as those of a growing adolescent. A dear aunt who lived in the United States wanted to help me and my family by bringing us to America. My aunt assured my parents that there would be opportunity and assistance for me to succeed there.

Me, my parents, my sister, and two of my brothers prepared to move to America. All of a sudden, I was to leave the only community I knew and understood. Despite all of the emotional pain I had suffered there, it had been my rock, my familiar world. *Will people be welcoming?*

*Kinder? More helpful? Will there be assistance and equipment to help me move about in that larger world, away from the small island on which I've been raised?* Although I knew that America had much more to offer in terms of helping me succeed, it was, nonetheless, a fearful thought to leave behind all that was familiar to me.

It was a frightening time, but it was also a period filled with curiosity and expectation. Here I was, ready to make the United States my new home, but I did not speak English. And though I was eager to start school and learn, I wondered if I had learned enough in São Miguel to be in the same class as others my age. *But wait, with my disability, will I even be allowed to attend school? And if I can, will the school be wheelchair accessible?*

I was twelve when we arrived in New Bedford, Massachusetts. My Aunt Isabel welcomed me and my family into her home with open arms. Her love and compassion was a comfort during this unpredictable transition. In addition to my family, God accompanied me on the journey. And despite the struggles I was sure I would encounter, I knew, with His love and His help, I would find my way to success.

It would be three months until my father would find employment and move us into our own home. My mother had to stay home and care for me. Meanwhile, my parents registered my brother and sister to attend school. During the course of interactions with the school personnel, my mother mentioned that she had a disabled daughter who also needed to be enrolled in school as well. Although education was mandatory in Massachusetts, at that time, schools were not handicapped accessible. How disappointing to find that I would continue to be left out of social interactions with classmates. Yet again, my education would be delivered through a tutor, this time only twice per week. Trade-offs seemed to be a constant in my life. I was grateful to be receiving my education through the process of home-schooling, but staying at home sustained and increased my sense of isolation.

As a pre-teen and then a young teen, I desperately wanted and needed a social life. If I was home schooled by choice, that was one thing. But I was tutored at home because there was no place for me in a public school. I wanted the same life that other teenagers had. I wanted to try new hairstyles for school, walk to the store for the latest music record hit, have a boy ask me out, and receive my first kiss. I wanted to feel what a broken heart felt like because at least that would mean I had been loved. Instead, I felt my heart ache with rejection—again. I would feel myself drift back toward the sadness I felt while living on the island. The looks on the faces of people who turned away from me reminded me of the pain and isolation that was too close to my heart. I couldn't help but feel ugly and invisible. The pain would often be immeasurable; when I listened to the unkind comments, crass words, and repeated declarations of how I would not achieve much in life; those words pierced me to my core. Little-by-little, the isolation and hurt chipped away at my confidence and self-esteem. Adolescence and puberty is already a difficult enough time in the life of a young girl. I felt, being in my body, that this time in my life was dreadful. Yet deep inside of me, I was determined that somehow, someway, I would be counted. *I will count!*

# Chapter 8:
# Holding on for Dear Life

*"If our hearts are ready for anything, we can open to our inevitable losses, and to the depths of our sorrow. We can grieve our lost loves, our lost youth, our lost health, our lost capacities. This is part of our humanness, part of the expression of our love for life."*

—*Tara Brach*

WHEN I WAS 18, I entered Lakeville Hospital in Massachusetts. My goal was to gain more able- bodied functioning so I could fit into society more easily. The doctors were trying to fit me with bilateral arm prosthetics so I could dress myself, as well as a prosthetic left leg to aid my mobility. I was there for a year and a half. Walking with the prosthetic was clumsy and very difficult. Learning to use the arm prosthetics was equally difficult. I had spent eighteen years learning how to get my body to work for me, and now someone was trying to convince me that the use of these artificial limbs would help. As I recall, I did not feel that these foreign limbs were helpful, especially the leg device. I was out of balance. But, true to form, I worked very hard to make this work—mostly because the doctors insisted this was what was best for me. I trusted them in their opinion that I would be "better off." This reminded me of the stories I was told as a child. After all, the doctors had assured my mother that I would be "better off" if I was dead. *What exactly does "being better off" mean when it comes to me?*

Back in 1973, prosthetics were made from hard plastic. They felt clumsy and encumbering, and I walked in an awkward way while wearing my leg prosthetic. The doctors at Lakeville Hospital decided that it would be easier for me to use the leg prosthetic, if I had my right foot amputated. They would then reconstruct my leg; my ankle would be my knee, and then the leg prosthetic would be attached to complete my leg. Their theory was that my stance would be more balanced and I would be able to walk better with two prosthetic legs instead of the one.

I was filled with a fear that sent chills down my spine. My foot was my tool. Using my only limb, my leg and foot, I could maneuver and reach. *How can I surrender the only usable limb I have,* I thought. I told my mother what the doctors had in mind. With an English translator, she came swiftly to the hospital. My mother was very strong that day and spoke with authority.

Once she had the facts, she made a decision. On my behalf, she declared that the amputation was not going to be done. I was so relieved that she had stood up for my best interest. I was young and naive to many things because, despite the doubts I had, I trusted the doctors' opinions. But with my mother's help and intervention, I was saved from the results of "what was best for me." I soon left the hospital and continued to do what I knew best. I used what God had given me and continued to learn how to function with my body just as it was. And I continued the search to find my place in the world.

# Chapter 9:
# Born for a Purpose

*I'm alone in the universe*
*So alone in the universe*
*I found magic, but they don't see it*
*They all call me a lunatic, okay, call me a lunatic*
*If I stand on my own, so be it*
*Because I have wings, yes I can fly*
*Around the moon and far beyond the sky*
*And one day soon I know there will be*
*One small voice in the universe*
*One true friend in the universe*
*Who believes in me.*

*—From Seussical The Musical, Alone in the Universe,*
*Based on books by Dr. Seuss*

I DISCOVERED THAT IN TIME of quiet, I could clearly see the duality in my life; I would find both peace and abandonment in solitude. But in my heart, I believed that somehow I would eventually be drawn to kind people who would help me reach my goals. For all the hurt and rejection, the kindness of the few outweighed the negative effects of the many others. This encouraged me to thrive. While each unkind act chipped away at my spirit, it also strengthened me. I knew I had to learn to be self-reliant and hard-working to achieve everything I needed to, if I were to have a valued life. And as I was determining my worth, deciding that I would be counted, I heard God reassure me. All along, I had kept to my faith in God and had made my Confirmation at Our Lady of Mount Carmel at the age of 14. Now, my heart and spirit listened to Him tell me that I was His daughter and that He had already counted me. He told me I was born for a reason and with a purpose. He also told me not to let cruelty blind me or limit me. Since it was often difficult for me to find peace amongst people, this message gave me an incredible inner strength. *Yes, I most definitely will be counted.*

At home, I diligently studied, as I had an immense desire to learn. Homeschooling from age 12 to 22 gave me a good educational foundation. I felt that I was living in a less sheltered world than the one I'd known prior. Due to many previous experiences, there was much hesitance on my part to know when to accept help or when to reject it. Slowly, I grew more trusting as people came to understand and accept me. I learned to humbly wait for people to help me. If I needed assistance, I would ask. If I could manage on my own, I would. Not everyone was unkind or startled by my appearance, so I had to be sure I wasn't pushing everyone away out of habit. Eventually, I learned to gratefully accept a lending hand. Rather than trying to be so self-aware and self-sufficient, I was now willing to accept offers of transportation, assistance in carrying items, and even the simple retrieval of a dropped pen.

One of my favorite teachers, Mr. Kimball, advised me to get my high school diploma. But I was already 22 years old. The usual inner battle raged inside of me. *How do I go about doing that? What will be the first step? Is it even possible?* It seemed that inner turmoil always reared its head when I set goals. These questions might seem easy for most people, but for me, action required much deliberation and risk-taking. Watching and listening to negative people taught me to value positive thinking. But on the other hand, if I failed, that would mean that those who believed that I couldn't accomplish something would be correct. Conflict accompanied me as I set my goals. I just wanted to prove people wrong. Unfortunately, that idea of proving naysayers wrong would become my obsession, eventually leading me away from my most important goal—to do what I, Filomena, wanted to do, and to do it for the right reasons.

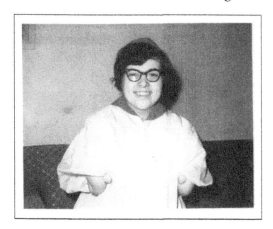

*Filomena at her confirmation*

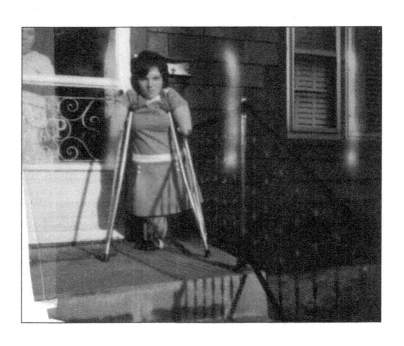

# Chapter 10:
# Dreams and Goals

*"We can improve our relationship with others by leaps and bounds if we become encouragers instead of critics."*

—*Joyce Meyer*

Mr. Kimball informed me of a night program at New Bedford High School, and then helped me to register. This teacher was a gift and an inspiration. Primarily, he believed I could succeed and achieve whatever I set my mind to. He probably never knew, but he brought my focus back to my own well-being. He showed me the value of learning for my own benefit rather than to prove to others I could be educated. I will never forget him for that reason; he opened an avenue of a much wider perspective forme.

I started to get excited about this positive opportunity. I knew my niece, Maria, would be available to help me with homework. She was very supportive and encouraged my success. Her voluntary support made my decision to attend night school that much easier. *With a good education, I can get a job and one day live on my own.* My mind swirled; optimism and ambition introduced new avenues of hope and possibility. *Maybe I can get a driver's license and even drive a car one day!* It was a wonderful relief to have dreams and goals in my life. This gave me a well-deserved and long overdue boost of encouragement and confidence to continue moving forward in life.

As I began my new adventure, it did not take long to meet challenges, much like in my past. Unkind, insensitive people intruded upon my positive moments. Being in my twenties, the pain of seeing people look away from me was very hurtful, even more so than when I was a child. I just wanted to be cared about for who I was as a person. I wanted to be able to style my hair, apply makeup, have a boyfriend, be pretty, and fit in with the rest of the crowd. Human desire builds naturally in our bodies and I was affected just like any other woman my age. I wanted to be loved, to be held, to be made love to, to marry, have children, and raise a family. It did not escape me that again, to take steps toward my success, I had to face rejection and cruelty.

I was transported to and from New Bedford High School for my classes by Massachusetts Rehabilitation Commission (MRC). It was arranged for the janitor of the high school to meet me and push me to my first class, and then to return me to the transportation area at the end of the night. Sometimes, he would get caught up in his work and forget to transport me to my next class; I then had to rely on another student or a teacher to come and transport me. And if he forgot me at the end of the evening's classes, I had to wait until someone located him.

Being forgotten like that would make me wonder, *Is it because I'm ugly, invisible, or both?* Doesn't everyone want to be understood, recognized, and appreciated? After all, those feelings symbolize basic human needs. I felt like carrying a sign reading, *I AM JUST LIKE YOU!* Everyone, not just the disabled, becomes emotionally depleted when they lack emotional ties or interactions. *Can't people see that although my body may be different, my emotional needs are the same as theirs?* The fact that I didn't have limbs didn't disqualify me from humanity, but sorrow and pain always seemed to track me down. I had to learn to thrive on a lot less than the average person. Like a cactus in the desert or grapes on a vine, both devoid of rain, they longed for nourishment much like I did.

Fortunately, about a year before finishing my education, I was able to obtain a motorized wheelchair. This was a much-needed boost to my independence. I no longer had to wait for someone to transport me around, or to risk being forgotten again. And proudly on June 19, 1981, at the age of 26, I wore a cap and gown and graduated with my GED. I was pleased, proud, and content that I had reached yet another one of my goals—despite any naysayers. My next huge milestone, December 8, 1981, came in the form of my driver's license. After much study and practice, I drove a customized van home from Quincy, Massachusetts where I had earned the right to drive. I had started receiving SSI when I was 18 years old; therefore, the MRC helped to modify the van that my brother had co-signed for me since I did not have any credit. What a liberating feeling to drive all by myself—nerve-wracking, but liberating! Driving myself everywhere meant more independence for me. This was yet one more accomplishment to prove that I could measure up to others' expectations and disprove their doubts.

Because of my circumstances, constant internal battles and persistent doubts fueled my determination to fit in. I had yet to find it within myself to ignore what others thought of me. I was full of my own fear, full of my own doubts, and I certainly didn't need to absorb others' negativity. Depending on the day, I had enough of my own negativity and doubt to battle.

Imagine a life where most days are spent proving to others that you are capable, valuable, and able. Imagine how exhausting it would be to struggle to learn the simplest of tasks such as eating, dressing, and writing. Things that most people take for granted can seem to be insurmountable challenges for others. I could have become resentful. And honestly, I sometimes was—secretly. Looks and stares hurt me. What people could not see ON my body caused them to be blind to who I was. In seeing what I did NOT have, people missed seeing all that I DID have—within my heart and my mind.

Only God knew me both inside and out, but he gave me life experiences that molded and shaped me into who I was to become. He knew my struggles. He knew my heart. He knew my loneliness. It was always challenging, but I refused to give up on God and He on me. He always sends someone to help;

someone to love us and appreciate us. I didn't know it then, but that someone was about to enter my life.

# Chapter 11:
# More Change

*"How it felt to have the world moving beneath me,*
*a hand gripping mine, knowing if I fell, at least I*
*wouldn't do it alone."*

—*Sarah Dessen*

Now that I had the independence of being able to travel about places on my own, I was determined to take the next big step and move out on my own. In 1982, I moved into a lovely apartment in South Dartmouth, Massachusetts. Solemar became my new home. My apartment was adorable and totally wheelchair accessible. I now had a large living room, a kitchen that met my needs, and even a porch located off the back door—all of it mine! I felt empowered since now I was the one who was totally responsible for my new home. I felt like life was beginning to treat me better, and I was grateful.

Up until this time, my mother and sister were responsible for taking care of me. They tended to all my needs, from dressing me to bathing me, and attending to my personal hygiene.

Now that I would be living away from home, a personal care attendant (PCA) was provided to me by the state. Even though I am an independent person, I knew that I still needed assistance with the tasks required of daily living.

I had been volunteering at a center for the handicapped for about a year. I found that my newly-found freedom allowed my personality to flourish. I also found my work very rewarding. I helped people learn to read English and to fill out important documents and applications. I even did crafts with them. This was a pleasant time in my life and it was going to get even better.

I met a man at the center who was also disabled and in a wheelchair. He was a handsome, caring man; his name was Luis. Although he was much older than I, we had much in common, and it wasn't long before we became very good friends. We continued to interact at the center.

Eventually, we began meeting in a more personal, social setting on a regular basis. People had taught Luis to be fearful, which limited his abilities. In many ways, he was afraid to live his life. Together, we helped each other gain our independence in many ways.

Here we were, both handicapped, and each of our mothers wanted to shelter us, to protect us from hurt and disappointment. But we were also normal. We each had a desire to share our lives with someone special. My mother would remind me that I was a disabled woman and questioned why I would want a man. I would then remind her that I was, in fact, a normal woman—no different in needs and desires. *Why would I be different from other women?*

Before long, we fell in love. I had dreamed of falling in love for so long, but I never thought it would really happen because words and actions toward me had distorted my self- image. We announced our marriage plans and, as usual, we were met with negativity. Our mothers felt that since we couldn't take care of ourselves, we would not be able to take care of each other. However, we actually had been taking care of ourselves and each other just fine. It was the fear of the unknown again, a barrier that had been restricting our lives for so long.

At 27 and very much in love, I married Luis Diniz, and we both lived in Solemar together. We loved each other very much. Luis was everything to me: husband, father, and friend. He was the gentle, protective male figure I longed for. A great peace filled my heart when I was with him. To be loved by someone who was not family felt so different. This man loved me unconditionally; Luis saw me for who I was. More than that, he saw into my heart and soul. He saw the person, not just the physical body. He didn't see what was missing from me; he saw all I was. To him, I was beautiful. His unconditional love affirmed that I was valued. We did everything together, enjoying life as much as we could, and it felt quite wonderful. We laughed together and we talked about everything. Luis listened to me. He heard my voice, my words, and my thoughts. I heard his as well, including all his hopes and dreams. This was as close to a balanced relationship as I'd ever known. To have a loving, intimate, and nurturing relationship with a man was more than I dared to dream possible. This was one of happiest times of my life.

Eventually, people changed their opinion and accepted our love and our marriage. We attended church together and were involved in many other social activities with family. We enjoyed our life together very much.

One Saturday morning in October, Luis sat with me at the breakfast table. We had plans for the day; we were going to celebrate my birthday. Luis loved my cooking and I was making his favorite meal—a boiled dinner. The pot was at a low simmer on the stove. The aroma of cabbage, onion, carrots, chourico, and pork filled our apartment. After breakfast, he excused himself from the table to get dressed. Time passed. *It is taking him so long,* I thought, and went to check on him. He was sitting, his eyes fixed and staring. When I asked what was wrong, he explained that his head was moving and that the bed was upside down. I thought it was the result of his high blood pressure. He asked for a glass of orange juice, which I scurried to get. Then he asked me to lie down by his side. I pushed up close to him. He seemed to be getting worse, so I told him that I was going to call his brother-in-law to come and help get him into his chair for a trip to the hospital. Instead, he asked me to stay with him, while he held me tightly by his side.

Tenderly, we hugged each other. But I had to leave his side to make the call. Upon my return, Luis' speech had gotten worse. Returning to his side, he gave me such a big hug, pleading, "Don't leave me."

Mario and his wife arrived quickly and called for an ambulance. Luis whispered to his brother-in-law that he knew he would never return home; he knew he was dying.

We had enjoyed seven glorious years together. On that day, my 34th birthday, Luis was stricken with a brain aneurysm. He was in a coma for one week before he died. The love of my life was gone. The man whom I adored and who had adored me, my friend, my husband, and confidant, was gone forever.

This was like nothing I had ever experienced before. The pain was deeper than any pain I had ever known. My tears came from the deepest, most vulnerable place in my heart. My whole life came crashing down around me. There was no way I was going survive this agony, this loss. My husband was gone. Nothing and no one could console my broken heart.

# Chapter 12:
# Ants and Agony

*"Loss doesn't feel redeemable. But for me one consoling aspect is the recognition that, in this at least, none of us is different from anyone else. We all lose loved ones; we all face our own death."*

—Meghan O'Rourke

LEFT NOW TO DWELL IN the darkness of my mind, my thoughts drifted back in time. My life had been difficult from birth. For as much as I had fought to be connected to the world around me, setbacks constantly challenged me. When I reflected on all the hard work I had exerted to do the things that many take for granted, my burden grew heavier. My mind continued its hurt-filled journey. I kept thinking about my life and all the losses I had known: loss of time, relationships, and opportunities. And now my heart was crumbling because of its greatest loss of all.

Every cell in my body was exhausted. I had struggled so long and hard to find my way and to show everyone in my life that I mattered. The fight within me was now gone. I had hoped for so long that I could take part in a normal life, but now my normal life, my life with Luis, was gone. My dear Luis was taken away too soon. He had dreams he had yet to realize. We were supposed to secure more joys from our life together. My rock was gone. My heart broken into pieces. Luis' life had come to an end and I was sorrowful for him. I felt pain and sadness that our love was broken apart, and I felt utterly destroyed at the thought of life without him. My painful thoughts repeated a mantra of sorrow and disbelief. *How could the man whom I loved and who loved me be gone forever?* I crumbled further upon remembering that my mother had been told— almost warned, it seemed—that this was no world for her child. This was just too much to bear. I no longer had the energy to force myself to survive in a life that kept knocking me down. There was no desire left inside me to continue for another moment. Depression and defeat coursed through my veins.

After the funeral, my cute apartment became a very lonely place—lifeless and empty. I did not want to live there any longer. My desire to live ended with Luis' death. The spirit that I had worked so diligently on growing and strengthening had accompanied Luis on his journey to God. He had great faith and I knew he was at peace in God's care. But that thought did not help me with my struggle here on earth. A crash brought me back from my reverie. On the nearby coffee table, a nearly empty bottle of Vinho Verde, a Portuguese white wine, fell over. I didn't care. *Let the crystal wedding glass shatter along with my life.* In my mind, all was lost.

In my thirty four years, I had proven many things to many people. I had been schooled, found a job, and drove a vehicle. But none of it meant a thing to me now. All of that effort had left me hollow, like a robin's egg invaded by a ravenous hawk. *Life has robbed me of too much—first my limbs and now my love.* If my tears had turned to blood and I had died on the floor, that would be just fine with me. I asked God why my life had to be like this, but I didn't even care if I got an answer. In truth, answers no longer concerned me. I now cared about nothing at all.

Though loved ones tried to comfort me, I was inconsolable. I was invisible even to myself now, broken of mind and spirit. *Nothing matters. Nothing at all.* Misery took Luis' place as my best friend. I turned away from everything in my life. My faith in God was distant and remote. All I wanted was for my mind to stop tormenting me with memories and for my heart to stop aching with pain. I had retreated to a familiar place—isolation. I knew that place well as a child; it was a familiar place to be. Once again, in this cruel and foreign world, I lived in myself-imposed cage, following a routine that I found to be predictable at best. Each day was dark, just like my soul.

I spent the next three years mostly in self-imposed seclusion. The days were mostly empty, with the exception of some loving family members who tried to help me. I spent most of my time drinking. Over time, that grew into a big problem. I convinced myself that I could not get out of bed in the morning without first having a drink. Thoughts of my lifetime of struggle just wouldn't leave me. The words, "*Tu nan podes fazer nada como os outros,*" was all I could hear. "You can't do it. You can't do what others do." Those words echoed in my mind, driving me crazy. For as much as I fought against those words all my life, they had now become my truth. I just didn't feel like I could do anything but drink. And I heartily believed the lie that I could no longer function without drinking.

Numbing my mind with alcohol was my survival plan. I truly believed that. To believe differently would mean I would have to get back to work, straightening out my life. That was something I did not want to do. I chose that for myself; no one forced this prolonged misery on me, except me. I felt cornered. My neighbors visited and I would end up being admitted to the hospital due to them calling an ambulance when they discovered how drunk I was. They had no kind words for me, as they did not understand the grief I was experiencing. I would go to my oldest sister's home on the weekends to try and get better. She and her family were very supportive. But when I returned home, I fell back to using alcohol to relieve my sorrowful burden. One day, I was so drunk that my niece, Maria, took me to the emergency room. I was out of my mind, hallucinating. I had so much alcohol in my system that to continue drinking would have meant death. But to stop meant I would experience withdrawal. My choices had boxed me into a disastrous situation. Sometimes people entrap us; more often, we do it to ourselves.

So here I was, once again, faced with what my life had become. Everything looked so hopeless; my mind was in tangles, my heart was broken, my body was sick, and my emotions were drained. I lived like this for three long years. One night, I found myself alone in my apartment, the rain of a brutal thunderstorm lashing against both my apartment windows and my raw, empty heart. I had cried myself out, nearly empty of tears. I sat on the floor, too distraught to get into my wheelchair and too broken to care. I kicked off my shoe and stared at the window, rain tearing down the panes almost as quickly as my tears were streaming down my face. I felt completely overwhelmed and cried out, "Nothing has ever worked out for me in this miserable life. Everything is lost!" Everything in my life had died with my husband. The death of my desire to live another moment accompanied him on his journey to God.

My head was pounding from too much wine and too many tears. Every part of my being ached with a pain like nothing I had ever known before. "Why did my life have to be this way?" I cried out. "God, why?" I didn't even want an answer. In truth, that was no longer any concern to me. I cared about nothing at all. I was angry at life, at God, and at all the people who had hurt me. I was angry with Luis for leaving me. He had told me many times that if he died, I should continue living my life. *Didn't he realize that would be impossible?* I felt like I absolutely could not carry on without him.

On this drunken night, I lay down and watched the room spin. I noticed a piece of carrot on the floor. There was a tiny ant crawling along. I thought, "I have to get rid of that ant tomorrow. I have no strength tonight." Then I remembered my childhood companions, the wall ants. Those little bugs had an interesting life. They showed me a good example of creatures that can live and work together in harmony. The wall ants were a sign of life to me. They represented unity, cooperation, and partnership. It suddenly came to my attention those ants' qualities were at the root of my fascination with them. This little ant on my kitchen floor was life. *I'm life. All life comes from God.* My time with Luis had actually strengthened **my** faith in God because Luis' faith had been so strong. I knew these things in my mind, but my heart and soul were barren. I was completely at the lowest point in my life. Yet, something inside me yearned for change.

Another ant crawled to the carrot on the floor, and then another. Their industriousness was fascinating. The wall ants of my childhood had built a successful community. Each ant seemed to know its place in their organized system. They each had a duty to perform. They seemed to do it with relative ease in unison with each other, doing their part, aiding in the survival of the entire colony of task. But why, on this particular night of darkness, were they crawling out from under the cabinet? I actually talked to the ants that night and confided that I, the broken human being, was ready to give up. I, Filomena, Friend of Ants, wanted to live in a community of mutual cooperation which would honor all life. I knew this was one of my deepest desires. And suddenly, my heart was warmed a little bit by a longing for something good to come to me once again. All the days of my life I had worked to be normal; but I was not the example of a "normal" person because of my birth defects. *But aren't we all unique in some way? Why must our differences overshadow our similarities?* Suddenly, the three ants retreated, out of sight, away from the carrot slice. I felt like I was saying goodbye to old friends.

Once again, my inner battle erupted. Beneath all the sorrow, I knew who I was and I knew my potential. Somehow, I had lost sight of it all. My husband's death had broken me, but I believe I was well on my way to falling apart prior to that. I felt that something very important had been missing from my life, but I had not been able to figure out what it was. What had I missed along the way that led me to this colossal agony?

I continued to lie on the floor, drunk and defeated. Cruel people and circumstance had finally won. Hopelessness and defeat stood strong as I fell. Out of complete desperation and loss of self-value, I cried out, "God, I cannot go on like this any longer. I beg you, please help me!

God help me." I was at my lowest point and I felt void, empty. I was afraid to live, yet I was also afraid to die.

Because my life was spent observing how others behaved, I had worked at being who I thought others wanted me to be. Never once had I looked deeply within myself to figure out who I was down deep in my heart and soul. I had not ever considered life on my own terms; instead, I'd wondered where I was supposed to fit into others' lives. I had played my role well in proving myself to people, but I was a stranger unto myself. That is where the real neglect had occurred. I had rarely asked myself what mattered to me; rather, I had moved through life trying to show people I mattered. As a result of that contradictory thought process, I had lost myself. The pain of that realization hurt deeply.

Just as I prepared to plead for God's help again, the telephone rang. I did not want to answer it. I did not want to pick up the line and risk that it was someone calling to make fun of me. I did not want to be told to get better. I did not want to face reality. So, it rang and rang.

Finally, I picked up the receiver; it was an automated call. The recording asked if I knew Jesus and if I was interested in a bible study. I almost disconnected the call, as I was so angered by the intrusion. Instead, I responded that "I would, in fact, like a bible study." I hung up the phone, feeling as if it had taken all my strength to say those few words. Yet the words had just flowed out of my mouth, almost against my will. "Yes" was the blessed word that would eventually transform me. Within a few minutes, the phone rang again. There was a man on the line responding to my reply. After a short conversation, I hung up the telephone. And for the first time in a very long time, I felt God in my apartment. Tears fell, as my heart softened a bit. *God has heard my plea.* In great agony, I had spoken to God, and He had heard me.

The desire to live began to flow through my veins again. According to Matthew 20:18, "Wherever two or more are gathered in My name, there shall I be." A stranger, by God's own grace, had reached out to me in a positive way; this felt like a miracle. Just by answering the phone and accepting a helping hand, the process of healing was set into motion. There had been so many times when I had not felt as if I'd been heard; something was different this time.

Answering the phone was the best thing I could have done that day. By saying yes to life once again, maybe life would say yes to me.

# Chapter 13:
# Finally—I See Myself

*"You cannot have a positive life*
*and a negative mind."*

—*Joyce Meyer*

A WEEK OR SO LATER, a young woman called me to arrange for a visit to my apartment where she could talk to me about God. After a few weeks of talking with her and building my trust, I told her what had transpired in my life. It was a wonderful relief to speak to someone who didn't judge me or make fun of me. That alone was a gift.

Several weeks later, I received a call asking if the pastor and his wife could stop by and visit with me. Once again, I agreed; this was my affirmation of willingness to get better. When I opened the door for them, I felt like I was seeing Jesus standing in the doorway, accompanied by two angels. I confessed all I had been going through, as well as the feelings I had been harboring for so long. I shared about the loss of my husband three years previous. Suddenly, it seemed almost incomprehensible that three years of my life had gone by, all spent in a fog of depression. In a way, time had stopped; circumstances, fear, and anger had held me captive like a caged prisoner. I had put myself into that cage and had thrown away the key. I had to be held accountable for my choices. Taking responsibility was my very first important step.

I had studied people all my life and learned how to function like them. It was life imitating art. I had spent so much time figuring out which people I should "be like," that along the way, I had neglected to follow my own heart and soul. Beyond my physical body, I had never looked deeply enough into myself to discover who I was. I had greatly neglected my spirit; I had not gotten to know myself. The person that God had created in His image was me, and what a beautiful creation I was. All my days had been spent proving I was worthy to be counted—by other people's standards, of course. Not my own. I hadn't taken the time to make sure that I counted—to myself.

The members of this church were people I could confide in. The relief of getting all the sorrow off my mind was uplifting. Relinquishing my pain, depression, anger, and remorse to people who did not sit in judgement was liberating. People were seeing me, hearing me, and caring for me; I felt loved. I could hear God telling me, "My daughter, you are counted in my kingdom. You are loved. You are more than you have yet to realize. Go forward." Over the last three years, I had abandoned by life. But now I was seeing that through it all, God had never abandoned me. He had always been with me.

My exhaustion had been borne of defense, my trying to

prove to people that I could do what 'normal' people could. My pain had grown from all of my losses: the loss of my husband, my dignity, my limbs, and my courage. What I lacked physically became my focus and that had completely distorted my view of who I was. I had always longed for the day when people would see past my invisible arms and leg and look at me, the person, not just my disability. But I realized that before people could look at me differently, I needed to view myself in a way I never had before. I hadn't loved myself at all. In truth, I had believed all the negative things people had said right along. It was the fear within me that perpetuated my need to continuously have to try to prove them wrong. I thought that if I could convince others, then I could convince myself. But I had it all backwards. I had to discover who I was, apart from my life experiences. This was the most important lesson of my life. Ever so slowly, I began to learn to care about and love myself. This was the beginning of the end of my lifetime of sorrow.

# Chapter 14:
# Make Love Your Aim

*"Darkness cannot drive out darkness:*
*only light can do that.*
*Hate cannot drive out hate:*
*only love can do that."*

—*Martin Luther King Jr.*

THE ACTION I HAD TAKEN by simply picking up the telephone that day turned my life around. For assistance to be useful, we must desire to be helped, and true lasting assistance must be invited into our lives. Barricading ourselves behind closed-off walls can lead to potential failure, even destruction. Human beings need each other to thrive; we must stay connected through the powerful belief that we are a part of each other's well-being.

The pastor invited me to attend church. I was never the same woman after that experience. God released me from all the hate I had for others. He lifted my burden of self-hate, too. The anger I had toward myself was my greatest burden. I was too hard on myself, always pushing and pushing, rarely grateful for who I was. All of that was gone forever. I fell in love with God. In doing so, God showed me how to love myself. I forgave myself for my weaknesses. I forgave myself for forgetting the importance of love. I released my bitterness.

This was a new experience. For as much as I had accomplished prior to my fall, I realized through it all that I had been too harsh on myself. I hated who I was; I hated the beautiful person God had created. I had been consumed with loathing and hatred for everything, including God. I believed the greatest lie of all: that I was not loved. I believed that I was not worthy of a good and decent life just because of my birth defects. Void of even the tiniest bit of compassion for myself, I finally saw that I had been invisible to myself.

Repairing my inner self was a priority. That was something that never occurred to me before. I realized that proving myself to people was a destructive dynamic that did not serve me well. Surrounding myself with people who accepted me and gave me room to grow as a person was essential. I set new goals, but I carried them out with a completely different attitude.

I now realized that in the early part of my life, my energies had been misguided. My view of what my life should have like was, until this moment in time, backwards. That was fine. I'd long since forgiven myself. Honestly, my experiences, good and bad, slowly molded me into who I am today, and I love who I am.

This time in my life reminded me of one other empowering event. When I was 21, I traveled to São Miguel with my niece to visit with friends. We were there for a month and we had so much fun. I felt free to explore and experience life. We laughed often and simply enjoyed ourselves. I wasn't accountable to anyone because I was surrounded by people who cared only for what was inside of me. This was one of the first times I felt empowered to live my life on my own terms. Here I was, experiencing that type of freedom again. Mature, happy, and strong, I was now ready to fully live life.

I knew I needed to live my life for me, guided by the God I loved and who loved me. I was joyful to discover what sustained me, as we all should; we must focus on our discoveries and reflect upon them in our daily living, so that we have something continuously nurturing us.

As I looked around my church, I realized that people, each with a different perspective, still had the same commonality. What we all had in common was the belief that everyone should be loved. The lack of perceived love can destroy a good life.

I was not defective. *It's just that my body looks different. I'm still a human being. I'm still a child of God.* God wanted me to see myself as His creation. Finally, my eyes were opened. I'd never imagined how debilitating anger could be, nor did I understand that underneath all that anger was a person who had been subdued by fear. This very same fear divides what God creates. I was now aware that things would come to me in a completely different way because my point of view had changed dramatically. For the first time in my life, I could look at myself and feel love.

# Chapter 15:
# A Second Chance

*"If you were born without wings,
do nothing to prevent them from growing."*

—Coco Chanel

IN 1993, I BEGAN TO regularly attend what is now called United Pentecostal Church. The people there were very supportive and loving; they were sincere. Once my faith began to flourish and I had matured, life turned around. I realized I had much to offer my community and beyond. I was no longer that little disabled girl from São Miguel struggling to find a place in the world. I was a grown woman who understood that my life had value. Living in accordance with that knowledge, my faith strengthened and God was my salvation. I had left all my negative thinking behind. I now looked at life differently. It was not about proving myself to anyone. It was now about living life to the fullest, respecting the life God gave me. Life for me was now about being engaged, proactive, and, most of all, reverent of life.

My new church was an active one, and I made new friends and forged solid relationships. One of our members was a gentleman by the name of James Tripp. Jim was a very bright spot in my life because of his kindness; he was a peaceful man who loved God. He mirrored what I had failed to see in my life. When Jim looked at me, he saw just me, my identity, not my disability.

Though he had some fears of his own, we somehow managed to find very healthy ground upon which to grow. We often ventured out together after church services; this progressed to dinners out and regular dates.

After many months of getting to know him, I discovered something was beginning to happen that I thought was impossible; I was falling in love. This time, love was something much different. I was a better person and much more in touch with my truth, better able to love in the right way and for the right reasons. I was better able to express who I was. I was growing as a person, more steadily than ever before. Jim and I reflected the best in each other and, as a result, something very special grew between us and through us. We spent more and more time together, enjoying drives to the ocean and walks in Plymouth, Massachusetts. The fresh air and nature's beauty filled our spirits. We were two grateful souls unfolding into a new life together, centered in love. Jim asked me to marry him. I said yes.

I remembered the inspirational words I had heard so long ago—"When you say yes to life, life says yes to you." I was getting another chance at love. Although I had said yes, there was still some residual fear within me. I was afraid Jim might find someone he loved more and would eventually leave me. My greatest fear was to be deeply in love and to be hurt. I knew I could not bring that mindset with me into my marriage, so I spoke of my feelings with Jim.

When we shine light on our fears, they tend to disappear. Jim reassured me of his love; I trusted him and his word because I knew him to be a good man. It was a blessing to know love once again. I was thankful to be a better person for myself and for this marriage.

On May 13, 1995, we were married. I never thought someone so special would come into my life, but he had. Jim felt the same way. We both saw each other at the depth of our being. For once in my life, I felt stable and on solid ground. Through a series of blessings, I had been healed from previous misconceptions. I loved who I was and the woman I was becoming. One of the first gifts I learned to understand is that true love is very empowering. My life experiences generated compassion within me. Life began to take on a new direction because I'd decided to change my way of thinking.

# Chapter 16:
# Compassion

*"Don't let the perfect be the enemy of the good."*

—*Voltaire*

JIM AND I HAD BEEN married for a few years and we were very happy. I continued to set goals for myself and strive to meet them—this time, with the correct intentions. This was a time for me to live life centered around objectives that defined the person I had become. My husband was a great supporter, as well as an enthusiastic advocate for me. He was never negative, nor did he diminish my strength by babying me. We began our relationship encouraging each other and continued to do so. Every day revealed new challenges, as well as new adventures. At midlife, I was happier than I'd ever been. I enjoyed going to work, earning income, and helping people overcome their struggles. I felt purposeful and productive; I was motivated to help others in need.

By 1999, I was working with people within the disabled community; I learned there are many forms of disability.

Physical, mental, and emotional impairments do not disqualify people from living the best possible life. I don't know how or why basic human rights had seemingly eroded within various systems, but I did know I was going to work hard to implement those basic rights for the disabled.

Years ago, agony and misery had broken my spirit, but love reconstructed me and delivered me to a better quality of life. I assigned value to the lessons and experiences of my life because they helped to make me a better person who could serve others. I understood what depression and failure felt like. I knew what it was like to struggle and to feel like nothing ever worked out. My darkest moment had become my light; I wanted to share that light with others in the disabled community. Through the example of my own body, God showed me the importance of compassion; I was more than willing to pass that on. I loved helping people see their value and worth. We are all human beings and we need to be seen, heard, valued, and loved in our wholeness. It's that simple.

# Chapter 17:
# Live to be Free

*"We are each of us angels with only one wing and we can only fly by embracing one another."*

—*Luciano De Crescenzo*

LIFE SHOULD HAVE ROLLED RIGHT along, keeping to the straight and narrow. I had been through enough in my life that one might think I should be more than happy to just sit back and enjoy what I had. After all, for the first time in my life, I was feeling fine with just being me, missing limbs and all. I was married to a man whom I loved immensely, and he did the same in return. By now, we had bought and moved into our own home. I had a job that I loved and valued. I learned that cloudy days did not necessarily bring storms, and storms do not always indicate disaster. Life's difficulties are challenging recurrences, but there are messages and lessons to be learned from them to help us better prepare for the next one. There were so many ideas and lessons to reflect upon and appreciate. But in true Filomena fashion, I felt it was time to move on down that straight and narrow path of my life, and see if I could widen it or maybe throw a curve into it. I had an intense desire to take a giant step outside of the box—a giant leap of faith. I needed to drive out the last bits of anger and resentment from my past; I wanted to eradicate those last fragments of doubt and fear that I could test life on my own terms for a change. Boldly, I decided to take that jump of faith—literally. I decided that I wanted to skydive.

# Chapter 18:
# When Outside the Box is Outside the Plane

*"The best and most beautiful things in the world cannot be seen or even touched. They must be felt with the heart."*

—Helen Keller

I knew that skydiving would be a real challenge, but life is full of challenges. I also knew that this experience would be truly risky. Although sensibility had not escaped me, I felt intensely drawn to do it. Of course, anything could happen up there, but we never really know what is next in our lives or where situations will take us. Life is full of uncertainties, so why not embrace those uncertainties? I just felt I had to take advantage of the truth that life changes can be liberating. What better way to celebrate that understanding and acceptance than skydiving? There was no other more exhilarating choice that I could make that would release me, once and for

Invisible Courage

all, from the fears I felt; the fears I put upon myself and the ones ingrained in me long ago by others.

As per usual, I was met with people telling me I could not skydive. I called several companies, only to hear one negative response after the other. The companies had their reasons for not letting me jump and I had to respect their decisions. However, past experiences told me not to accept a "no" so easily anymore. Those negative answers flooded me with my past feelings of defeat and the struggles that had surrounded them. Therefore, my quest continued. Finally, I found a company in Lebanon, Maine that would accommodate me.

I explained my disability and they were willing to work with me. Doubtful, I went on to express to them the need to see me and to be completely aware of my limitations. After all, I wanted to skydive, but I didn't want to die. Again, they assured me; they had the proper staff and equipment to take me up for a jump.

I prepared with a coach. I was in a jumpsuit, all buckled up, ready to jump. As I sat in the plane, ready to be thrust out into the open air, memories of my life swept through my mind. As the plane rose higher and higher above the clouds, I continued my evaluation of the risk involved. I did not feel as though I was tempting fate. I knew accidents could happen, mistakes could be made, and errors in judgement exist—that's life. After all, we're imperfect humans.

This decision had been a huge stretch for me. But as I reviewed my life, I felt at peace with the experience. I knew my family was on the ground cheering me on. I looked down to

82

the earth which was more than twelve thousand feet below me. All I could see was the white tops of billowy clouds. This small, old plane in which I was being transported acted as a perfect metaphor for my life. The clouds represented all the ups and downs and walls I had walked along, walked through, and climbed over. As I left the plane, I was going to break free of the confines—not just those of my mind, but also of my body. The unknown can be frightening, but this venture was not. The anticipation was wonderfully exhilarating.

We jumped. I gasped. My lungs filled with air. My pulse raced. We fell from above the clouds. White billowy puffs of what looked like soft pillows were under me. Rapidly descending through the clouds, the mist of the white puffs refreshed my face, moistening my skin. It felt like a baptism of sorts. God created this beauty. *How glorious,* I thought. In a flash, we were beneath the clouds. Below was the earth. I looked down, everything looked so small, tiny, unassuming.

From this perspective, things looked manageable, almost welcoming.

The wind pushed against my body. It was exhilarating to watch the ground change in appearance, as I quickly descended. I had no fear in me. The images of trees and roadways grew larger and put my life into perspective. The idea came to me that everything was connected in some way. The trees to the dirt, dirt to the roads, cars to streets, houses to land, people to the ground. These related objects looked so tiny from up in the sky. But it all appeared to be woven together, like a fine tapestry. *What a spectacular treasure I'm witnessing,* I thought.

Falling at a speed of about one hundred and twenty miles per hour, I was experiencing what I felt was a miraculous transformation. I couldn't talk. I couldn't hear. I found such peace, as I sped toward the earth below; I had almost forgotten that my coach was buckled in with me. I was free-falling, viewing the landscape for miles and miles; it was as though I was flying. I had missing limbs, but up there, it felt like I had wings. I don't think I've ever felt so free. Though I knew these could possibly be my last moments of life, I was alive and vital at that moment.

As the land rushed closer and closer and the wind blew in my face, my heart beat faster as excitement swept over me. I was all smiles, as I neared closer to the earth's surface.

Everything on the land got larger, as we continued our descent. I looked in all directions, scanning the horizon. I was happy and excited at the same time.

This jump broke through all the false beliefs and fears I'd ever accepted as my own.

*Anything is possible!* So much to process and appreciate in just one minute of free-falling. But then my coach pulled the parachute cord and we were thrust upward a bit. With the parachute open overhead, we slid through the air with gentle ease. It was as though we were floating through another world, calm and free from influences. I was so focused on the skydive that I did not give anything else much thought. There, up in the heavens, I was free; I felt incredibly calm and peaceful. And this quiet time of reflection brought forward a realization that had almost escaped me.

From my vantage point up in the air, I found true enlightenment. The tiny images on the ground reminded me once again of my childhood friends, the wall ants. *How could those little creatures still be so ingrained in me?* The tiny colony of life showed me the value of all of creation and the sacred connection we all share. Their united arrangement, a work in harmony, was a representation of the life that seemed so removed from me as a little girl, and even into my adult life. Time and time again, I had reflected on those cooperative insects, marveling at their apparent teamwork. But it was not until I was skydiving, experiencing a lifting of my own spirit, that I fully understood what the wall ants in my humble home in São Miguel were trying to show me.

The lesson I had learned from the ants was the same one I was getting while skydiving. I had watched the ants objectively as a little girl; I didn't judge them. I had no emotion invested in them. I simply observed. I did the same while I was skydiving; I simply observed what was around me. If we observe objectively, we do not cloud our situations with emotion. Instead, we just watch and draw from it what we must. I didn't have to judge the behavior of the ants or manage them in anyway. I didn't have to analyze the ground below, as I fell through the air. All I needed to do was acknowledge it. I saw the ants, I saw the landscape, and I saw my family in the distance. Everything was before me and I wasn't judging any of it.

When my coach pulled the cord to release the parachute, it was as though it released all my past pain, fear, and hurt into the air. My former feelings were passed to the angels for safe keeping, held in love. I could be objective now. I no longer needed to be knotted up in what had been in my past. All I needed to do was give thanks for my life, humbly and without judgement.

Faster and faster, we were hurled toward the ground. I could see my husband and family waiting for me to land. But at that moment, I felt like I was on a swing high up in the air. This was the most liberating experience of my life. Finally, we landed safely, with me sitting on my coach's lap. All I could do was scream, "I did it! I did it! I did it!" My coach laughed, as I continued to rejoice at this success. Everyone was smiling and cheering. Five minutes of pure ecstasy. *I am alive!* My entire body quivered with happiness. "I did it! I did it!" As my smiling family ran toward me, I continued to shout that joyful chant.

Sometimes it is the simple, quiet moments in life where the smallest realizations cause the largest impact. Peacefully sailing through the clouds in a free fall was one of the most sacred moments of my life. I truly felt close to God in the heavens. The quiet up there was like being in deep prayer. In the relatively short time I was skydiving, I was very close to The One who created me; I realized I had been with God all along. Here I was, no arms and only one leg, yet I flew. The air felt pure in the wide-open sky. Both my heart and soul were filled with an abiding sense of love. As I fell nearer to the ground, I recalled the silent whispers from God and the angels, "Filomena, you are loved." Those whispers led me to finally realize that I needed to love who I was.

On my descent, I looked out over the terrain to see the

tree tops, the various shades of green and brown, the blue sky above, a field of lavender. My flight to the ground was like a sparrow falling from its nest, only to discover it is more than able to fly. And I also discovered a universal truth: God is Love, and God loves all that He created. *Therefore, God loves me.* A feeling of warmth enveloped me. My arms felt like wings. As my lungs filled with fresh air, I thought, *Filomena, I love you.* In that moment, I was free forever. It was never about proving to others who I was; it was about believing in myself and realizing I am blessed. It wasn't about declaring what I could do, but rather me declaring love is powerful. That skydiving experience was just long enough for me to review my life. And seeing my family run to me warmed my heart. Jim led the way, and when he got down on his knees to greet me, I looked in his eyes and he into mine. He knew of all my struggles. When I said, "I did it," he knew exactly what I was referring to. Skydiving that day was so much more than a jump from a plane, and the fact that he knew me so well was a gift like no other. I was heard, seen, valued, and loved just as I was. This excursion brought me home, finally and completely. Home for me was being comfortable with who I was and who I had become. It was being able to love myself unconditionally. And I do.

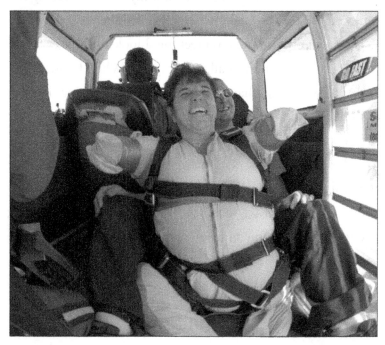

# Reflections

FOR MANY YEARS, IT TOOK a great deal of courage for me
to move around in society. That, alone, was challenging. That
is likely a result of the fact that people with disabilities were
far removed from mainstream society. The average person was
not exposed to individuals with handicaps and, when they saw
someone that looked or behaved differently, it was startling.
Some people felt my willingness to be out in public was an
example of courage and determination; others thought it was
appalling. But deep inside, I felt there was a world to experience, people to meet, and plenty to accomplish. But much like
everyone else, I had a list of goals to meet, and I refused to give
up on them and spend my life in hiding.

Even today, there are some glaring illustrations of division
in our society; the rich versus the poor, the healthy versus the
ill, and the disabled versus the whole are just a few. But divided
communities and families fall apart. Individuals divided against
themselves are doomed to fail. I, too, was divided, even within
my own heart. My inner world was a battlefield of bitterness
and anger. But it was I who needed to change my intention
and perspective. I was the one who had sent my world crash-

ing years earlier. No one did that to me except me; my choices marked my path. To look at the world with hatred because of a handicap demolishes the best of who we can become. Our own accountability must be at the forefront of attaining successful, balanced lifestyles. To point fingers is counterproductive. Instead, we must search—some more than others—and seek out ways to build productive lives despite what we perceive is a "missing" piece of ourselves.

Everyone can relate to a time in life when they were made to feel invisible. On my life's journey, I endured those times all too often. When at a supermarket or a clothing shop, accompanied by a friend, the clerk would address my companion instead of me. "What would she like to order?" "Ask her," they would say. It is fear and lack of understanding that makes people act this way. But I understood. Nonetheless, these were examples of my invisible moments and they were extremely frustrating. I had to shift in the wheelchair, sit a little taller to be seen, and then I would answer their questions. The fact was that my appearance frightened people. Although I learned to be more assertive, time-after-time people would look the other way. I exemplified the stereotypical images of disabled people. No arms meant I couldn't hear. No leg meant I couldn't see. And a wheelchair apparently gave permission for people to look away.

I may have been invisible to some people, but my feelings, dreams, and desires never vanished from my mind. Observing people, I thought, *I see and hear you. So why is it such a struggle for you to see me?* Sometimes their reactions prompted me to giggle. *Do they think I don't know how I look? Do they not want to look at me, so I won't notice that my arms are missing? What frightens them?* Fear became the major wall to break through.

We have much more control over our destinies than we give ourselves credit for. With each decision, we choose our direction. I was amazed to realize how much my attitude and thought process shifted when I began to love myself. For the first time in my life, I felt at ease. The battle was extinguished by love.

I still reflect on the time I was a little girl playing with the wall ants. All these years later, their tender message is secure in my heart. I could not have known then what that colony would eventually mean to me. I first needed to pass through my own struggles. Those ants lived in harmony, collaborating and purposefully functioning as a unit. They all needed each other on some level to build their environment. My tiny toes had dug for a truth that took decades to recognize. Somehow, that truth stayed with me all the days of my life. This gentle and powerful lesson was a gift to me. As a toddler, I was confused and ignorant of what I was witnessing within that wall, but I carried the lesson with me until I matured enough to recognize it. That simple lesson is—love life.

My eyes water a bit, as I reflect on this moment in my life. Humanity is much like the colony of wall ants that I played with. We truly need one another. We need to be the best we can be with each other. The works in our lives—whether it be in families, schooling, or careers— need to be centered on a beneficial coexistence. The differences we see in one another do not have to be, nor should they be, the blocks to dividing walls. Instead, we should be building bridges. Differences are not at our physical cores; we must reach the love and compassion we are destined to share with others. This is the goal that really matters.

Life had been molding me like the earth crushes coal and turns it into a diamond over time. Now was the time to break out of the box, once and for all, and to shine. We create the cages we live in, that much I know for sure. I did not create my disability, but I did nurture the point of view that prevented me from growing into a productive and balanced person. To be the best person I can be, I am always learning and trying to improve myself. Doing that which makes me the person God created is more liberating than becoming a person who wants to prove something to others. If I count, and I do, I count because it is a declaration from God, and I humbly honor that. At the end of each day, I have to be able to live with who I am and know that I am trying to please God. I need to be all I can be and use that in service to others. That is what I learned after hitting rock bottom; my darkest moment became my light.

# Invisible Courage

by Janine Ouellette Sullivan

*When the only tool you have*
*is your heart*
*worn on your sleeve*
*and your dreams placed on your soul*
*that conceive a destiny unmatchable.*
*When invisible hands reconfigure views*
*a smile quells fear*
*bold language sets those in a cage free*
*and the unseen shines a light of hope*
*room appears for the disenfranchised,*
*we all rise up together.*
*when choice leads the way*
*love sets a clearing*
*we hear the call to continue*
*to the best we are able and know*
*days well lived bring forth*
*invisible courage made visible.*

# My Message

AFTER SKYDIVING, I MET A man by the name of Roberto Medeiros. He lived in São Miguel and was in the area on business. Although he remembered me, I did not recall having met him previously. He shared his recollection with me. He had been on his way to a celebration in one of the villages. He had money which he intended to use to buy candy. Instead, he became a donator at one of the feasts my father had brought me to. Here, all these years later, we were speaking. He asked me if I would consider traveling to Portugal to speak to people who had various types of disabilities. He wanted me to share my personal story with people who had emotional, mental, and/or physical disabilities. Of course I agreed, as it had been a goal of mine to share my story with as many people as I could, hoping to inspire them. It is important that people with disabilities know there is a place for them in society.

Two years after that meeting, Roberto made it possible for me and my husband to travel to São Miguel. This was a dream come true. I was excited but anxious, as I didn't know what to expect. I was scheduled to speak at three conferences. The first conference had one hundred people in attendance. I explained to Roberto that I did not know how to speak in Portuguese in a professional style. He simply told me to speak from my heart. So, I did. At the second conference, there were many people as well. The attendees had cerebral palsy, were homeless, or had other difficult and different situations; they were all there to hear my story.

The third conference is the one I will never forget. There were five hundred children sitting in the conference center, waiting to hear me speak. I had brought donated walkers and wheelchairs, as these types of medical equipment were still quite scarce in Portugal. A mother approached me with her son who walked awkwardly on crutches. "If you ever receive a donated motorized wheelchair, could you send it to my son?" she asked. All of the children in attendance were special, but this young boy touched my heart. I could see he was brilliant; all he needed was to have a way to get around and explore his corner of the world and perhaps even beyond. *When I return home, I'm going to try to locate a motorized wheelchair for him.*

I gave my talk; not one child squirmed or made a sound. I was amazed at how attentive the children were. They were so inspired to see me and hear about my life. I believe I gave them hope. When I left, the children gathered at the windows and waved good-bye. I wept with joy at the thought that I had given them some hope for their futures. But I also knew that those children had given me far more than I gave them. I had found my mission, my calling.

We learn so much through the innocence of children. They respected me during that talk. In turn, I showed them how to have courage and how to respect the beautiful people they are. I shared with them the hurt and pain that people had inflicted upon me with their negative and often cruel words. I wanted the children to understand that they did not have to believe the falsehoods that other people might attempt to put upon them. I warned that if they believed the negative words, those ideas would get inside them, and they would build their own prisons from those words. After all, that had been my own story for so long, and I wanted them to avoid the path I had taken in believing what I shouldn't have. I wanted them to know they were gifts in this world and that they needed to believe that with all their hearts.

Roberto gave me a very important gift by arranging these speaking engagements. It was one of the first times I saw clearly that I needed to be very honest about my life story—publicly. My mission was, and still is, to help people with disabilities. Beyond that, I felt called to help people understand that they know their own heart best. I want to instill the message that they must not believe the negative comments or the negative messages that people try to put upon them. That continues to be my message.

I learned so much during my life and revisited each step as I wrote this book. I have discovered that daily self-review is a very important practice in nurturing body, mind, and soul. Because I had to look at life more deeply just to figure the mechanics of it all, I learned how to look at myself and others more deeply.

The toxic anger that had grown in my heart became the

catalyst for compassion and understanding. When others attempted to erode my qualities of self-esteem, confidence, and self-worth, I was able to recognize those patterns and guide others in finding ways to reverse that and gain back a positive self-image. It was later in life when I understood that the negative responses from people had more to do with their thinking and little to do with mine. I also learned that my negative reflections and responses to life was destroying me.

My story may be different from yours. However, I believe that what is common to all of us is the understanding that we gain so much of ourselves by valuing life and striving to enjoy it. When I stopped owning what was not mine in the first place, I began the practice of adhering to my personal truth.

As I wrote the pages of *Invisible Courage,* I sometimes cried as I revisited the pain I had experienced along the way. At other times, I felt angered and saw that there was still a tiny residue of resentment within me. Today, in my sixties, I am still learning how to be the best person I can be—not in spite of my life experience but because of it.

My work has focused on razing the barriers that block disabled people from living in mainstream society. After all, life is for learning and discovering one's place in the world, not sitting on the sidelines due to misunderstandings or lack of information about the disabled communities that struggle every day. It took many years, but I found my voice and I am an advocate for those who have not yet found theirs.

Life is for learning, discovering our place in our corner of the world—and for growing. Even now, once and for all I find

I'm ready to release lingering outrage over experiences I have known. To hang on to pain and hurt destroys what beauty that longs to be manifested through us.

My greatest lesson came to me after I hit my lowest point. I needed to love myself unconditionally. For me, that was the beginning of a life well lived. To loath who I was became the largest and deepest wall I could have ever constructed. This hatred of self caused me to be unable to love my God. My hope is that each reader will look within and realize the blessed gift you are, while also remembering to love other people. For me, loving others stunted the growth of my heart and the openness of my soul. When I felt I had no one, someone came to me. When I felt abandoned, someone came to me. When I fell, someone lifted me up. When love seemed distant, someone loved me. When I looked, I found. This is the miracle of life.

I knew it was time to speak about life as a disabled woman, so that my personal experience can help people achieve the life they were created to live. I am a human being with dreams, hopes, and desires. Yes, I was born with stump arms that did not develop from the elbow to hand. In addition, only one of my legs formed. Yet, I learned over time that who I am is much more important than those impairments. My physical appearance is only one part of a whole person. We are all born with a spirit that longs to meet our highest potential. I believe it is that yearning that drives us forward.

At some point in life, hopelessness comes in many forms. My desire is to lift the veil of defeat and shame from those struggling in life. This feeling of not belonging fools us into thinking that we do not have a place in this world. We are called to self-discovery, to seek ways to find our place in the life we have been given. Life holds many lessons; be curious about who you are and what your personal worth is.

Even now in my sixties, I often reflect on various events in my life. Some days were pleasant; some were very painful. I strongly believe that all of my life has been a gift. All of the people I have met along the way played a role in who I have become, which leaves me in awe of the mystery of life. Of course, no one wants to be born with any sort of disability. However, we must look for ways to overcome obstacles, or we will be defeated. Though there were plenty of times that I did feel quite crushed by life, the hope of something greater than defeat pulled me forward. I am truly thankful to all the people who have loved me unconditionally along the way, lifting me up to be the best person I can be.

I am still eager to discover the gifts that God has in store for me. There is always something purposeful to pursue; I encourage you to move to the next section of my book and begin your personal quest to be a shining light for yourself and others. Lifting each other up lessens the weight of negativity and increases our own joy.

## Postscript
# What Invisible Courage Means to Me

THESE DAYS, I LOOK BACK over my life and I ask myself, *How did I do that?* By *that* I mean a multitude of actions that lead me to this moment in my life. *How did I survive being born in 1955 on a simple island in the Azores when doctors neither believed I would live or should live? How did I learn to be self-reliant?*

I'll be honest; there are times even now when I speak of my story that all the feelings of hurt, rejection, and ridicule bubble up within me. Every now and then, a small dormant volcano of old emotions erupts in the gut of my being. I lift my half arms up and declare my story with a conviction that I was born to live my life well in spite of the countless obstacles. I catch my anger even now once it fills my heart. I catch it when the tone of my voice becomes harsh and I feel my blood pressure rise.

I catch myself thinking about the past, as if it were happening now. *I'm human after all. How many times have I had to say this sentence? How many times have I had to remind people of that? I'm human after all. I am here on the earth, in this body, living this life for many reasons.* In many ways, my birth defects did define me. But not in all ways. I am more than what is missing. I remind myself of that all the time. I am enough as I am. This was the most difficult thing to embrace, a strong sense of self.

As I've passed through the years working in the field of social service, I realized that many people—regardless of what they have or what they have done—struggle with feelings of inadequacy. Something is robbed from us at a very early age. Perhaps it is confidence or the understanding that we have the power to grow daily into the best we can be. Somewhere along life, an interior wall is built between the lies we believe about ourselves and our unique and personal truth.

I often think about the ants in the brick wall. I cannot help it. Even now, I'll be reminded of my play time at the patio wall at my home in São Miguel. I remember the patient little girl who dug with her big toe into the crevasse between each brick to figure out where the little ants came from—and what life meant. That one situation in my life told me more than I could have ever imagined. As a child, I did not understand the symbolism of the patio wall and the community of ants. There was, however, a sense of peace I found while playing at the wall that stayed with me. I was probing for answers.

When I was much older, I saw that each brick was an aspect of life, a person, a situation. The cement between the bricks that I so eagerly tried to dislodge represented the mistruths that build obstacles together in what looks like something impossible to overcome.

I had to learn to use my mind and body in such away that I could live a full, independent, and productive life. I had to seek ways to function in life with what I had and that did not come about by obsessing over what I did not have. That was my battleground, the space between can and can't, do and don't, succeed or fail, love or hate, live or die. There it was, every minute of every day.

What my body physically looks like was always the first thing people saw. I am a mirror reflecting something we all do—judge others. You can not judge me by my missing limbs. Yes, see what I look like, but don't leave it there. If you do than you will miss knowing who I am within. That fact can be applied to everyone. If you see someone of a different race, you cannot end the meeting there if you hope to overcome racism. If you meet someone of a different religion than yours, it is the time to learn more about that person and their beliefs.

In a world where division is deeper than ever, we must all find ways to dismantle these barriers we've built between each other, our cultures, and our countries. In my view, it is our main mission to find the common ground that we can stand on and have healthy, thriving relationships with one another.

For a long time, I felt my life was much harsher that most. As I matured, I realized my life experience impacted me much more than it did other people. I must come to grips with my personal experience.

People view their lives by how it effects them personally. We feel the grief of all kinds of loss and pain. Our pain is ours to experience and we must. No one can feel another's personal experience like they do. The gift comes forward when we look to move beyond a point of defeat and climb toward an improved life.

As I wrote this book, I have learned so much reviewing my life. I see how we all have a story that needs to be shared. Even now, while writing these pages, I'm reminded of situations I'd forgotten and people I had not thought about in a very long time, yet who had an influence on me.

Once again, I reviewed my pain to fine tune who I am now. I had not intended to write another word in this book until I realized that I am still growing and learning. That is what life is all about.

When I went skydiving, I knew I was doing something so bold it was sure to put an end to any lingering patterns of behavior that were not serving me well. The jump did just that. As I descended to the ground, for a few seconds I imagined that this could be my last moment. I asked myself, *What do I want to see, think, and feel right now?*

I wanted to feel the joy of my choice to live life well. That is what I wanted and that is what I did while flying through the air, looking at the broad view and finally seeing my loved ones waiting for me. If this was my last moment then I wanted to live it truthfully, deeply, and joyfully.

I understood that I always had an opportunity to observe my pain and sorrow. But I did not have to remain in that anguish. Obstacles were a part of life. To me, they were there to overcome. I would not be a brick builder in my own life.

My career has shown me that. People I work with need help to overcome their struggles. I needed help all along the way. That is what life is about. We are called to help one another overcome and rise up to the best we can be in the life we have been given.

I learned and believe deep in my heart that God has a very big and glorious dream for each of us. We have the choice to engulf ourselves in the dream God has for us, or wither in defeat and despair.

Awful things happen to us. Life can be that way. These are not punishments. It is how life unfolds for the greater purpose.

I discovered I was not born this way for some kind of punishment. I was born this way— period. I chose to accept what had been given and to glorify God. I chose to utilize my life to the best of my ability.

We all have many callings in life. My first calling was to accept who I was and love myself. At 37, I could not defile what God had created in me one more day. I realized God loved me. What was missing was that I did not love myself. Actually, I hated myself and conducted my life based on that. When my personal truth began to awaken within me, I saw life differently.

What I had not realized was life was preparing me for that moment all along.

Everything I tried to do had to be looked at in a different manner than someone with all their limbs would have looked at the same thing. Our perspectives were different. One wasn't right or wrong, good or bad—just different.

I had to look at a fork differently. *How can I hold it?* A door knob was an obstacle. Try to peel an orange with no hands. I had to look at that orange with a inquisitive eye.

Today, I thank God for the years I spent trying to prove to people I could do things. Even that was a gift. If I did not get angry enough to show people what I could do, I'm not sure I would have pushed myself so hard. That friction in my life was grace in action. It caused me to aim higher and strive to accomplish things. My intention was not necessarily wrong. My thinking was just a bit off. But my desire to learn more and do more was based in a desire to liberate myself from fear and lack.

We begin our struggles at different points based on our awareness of ourselves and the circumstances at the time. We do the best we can with what we have learned at that point. All I knew as a child was my effort to fit in with the normal kids would prevent me from feeling as lonely as I did.

It was in that loneliness that gave me incredible insight and a vision to be more. Needing to give so much attention to everything shaped my viewpoint and left me with a keen sense of how things work. For example, when I drive a van, there are a series of mechanical things just to get into the driver's seat. The ramp is lowered, I place and secure the wheelchair, then transfer to the driver's seat. After that, there's another batch of mechanics to apply my arms and leg properly to drive. I need to give attention to each one of those steps before I start the engine.

Life is like this, if we choose it to be. The more we give things attention, the more present we are to those things. The same holds true with people. In my work servicing people with disabilities, I give them my attention. I need to hear beyond their words what their need is. Some people arrive to the office panicked. They may have emotional, mental, or physical issues that complicate their life. Giving attention to them, I begin to understand their need more clearly and can help in a more productive way.

My own life taught me how to see people more clearly and to listen more deeply. When I pass by someone and do not receive eye contact, I already know a lot about that person. By my own life experience, I know I have met someone who is afraid to look at a handicapped person. That person may be asking themselves, *What do I say?* I am not really all that different that anyone. Other's are not all that different than me. We have our unique qualities, varying features, quirky ways. Underneath the superficial descriptives we are very similar.

I had to learn that about myself in order to thrive. I spent many years believing my appearance made me different. My body was different. Even though that was true, I was a human being worthy of common decency. This is everyone's right. If we could do just that one thing, I believe we would create a multitude of positive changes in our corner of the world.

Now in my sixties, I know a few things for sure. My God loves me, the quality of the attention we give to people and situations decides the direction the experience will flow in, and the first step in living a good, productive, and purposeful life is to love yourself first.

The love we hold in our heart is what guides us. In the early part of my life, I did not love myself at all. I was actually very hateful and bitter. I was angry at my parents, community, and even God. *Why did I have to struggle so much? Why did I have to look this way?*

I have learned over the years that my birth was part of a plan. I trust that. When I decided to love myself as I am and for who I am, I began to understand that I am part of a plan, a weaving of a life full of purpose.

Each step of the way, I need to make choices, physical choices—like, *how on earth can I do this?* Emotional choices like, *shall I love or shall I hate?* The choices of my heart and soul were invaluable to me. The physical challenges fine tuned my abilities. Overcoming emotional hurdles strengthened me. Tuning into my heart and soul has shaped me into being truly a whole person.

This is the main reason I wish to share my story. *What is a whole person?*

I suppose the answer to that question varies. For me, accepting myself and truly loving who I am helped a great deal in dealing with situations along the way. When I realized that the anger and hatred I felt was actually a result of my negative view of myself, life began to turn around for me.

It was also the kind and decent people I met, who accepted me as I was flawed, that showed me the way to self-actualization. Their actions opened a door in my heart that was refreshing.

Kindness, peace, and love feel much better than the opposite. Once I was able to lighten my burden through the help of others, my personal opinion of my role in this life changed. I never really had to prove anything to others. I just simply needed to see my own worth.

My true *invisible courage* was realizing the value I had within me all along. It was that part of me that consistently grew throughout my life. Some call it spirit, soul, heart.

Whatever word we use to describe that deep part of ourselves that drives us forward and higher with each experience, that is what we must harness.

When I understood something, I moved with it. When I learned how to write, I wrote.

When I learned how to drive, the world opened up for me and I drove. Most importantly, when I learned how to love myself as I was, all corners of my life improved. I then learned how to love other people more sincerely.

Invisible courage is the qualities we possess but are not seen until we dare to let our best self emerge. This is what improves our environment. Kindness toward self and others, this is the invisible courage. Loving others is invisible courage.

When we bring our strengths forward and fearlessly use them—especially in difficult situations—we bring what is invisible within us outward, and then the fruit of that positive action can be seen.

This, too, is a choice. I could have turned out completely different. I could have grown into a very bitter woman. When I was in the mindset of anger and fear, I could have stayed there.

I had plenty of people around me who would have supported that. We must shine light on darkness. This is what humanity is called to do.

I wanted more for myself. Independence and education liberated me. Interacting with diverse people expanded my point of view. The more of life I experienced and the more I learned to find my place in society, the more I involved myself in life and became a valuable part of society.

I had something important to contribute. My handicap did not alter that fact.

It took me nearly four decades to get myself on steady ground. As I met other people, I realized most people move through their life and gain insight as the years roll forward. Looking back and recalling being at the rock bottom of my life at age 37 didn't sadden me any longer. I speak to many people who tell me that they did not begin to understand who they were until they passed through difficulties and matured into their selfhood.

I deeply understood that being born without limbs made my life more challenging. That was for certain. But there has always been an entire part of who I am that dwelled in the wholeness God wishes for us all.

I have found the common ground with people, but I had to love myself first.

Had I not realized all that I had, I would have continued to look at the world and people around me with great suspicion.

We don't altogether realize how freeing it is to love ourselves. The burden is otherwise very heavy. To me, the greatest burden is fear. We cannot move forward, if we carry fear with us. The many blessings that I am aware of in my life are incredible. I am still in awe of the fact that I even lived past infancy, a miracle in many ways.

I heard a story about a little girl who was dying of cancer and was close to death. She opened her eyes and said, "I have a lot of living left to do." Her health began to improve after that declaration.

I don't know how much longer the little girl lived, but her words penetrated my spirit. Something that was otherwise invisible within her was verbalized and certainly inspired her family. That action altered her future. That is love and hope in action, invisible courage.

Those kind of qualities must be made visible by our actions.

I had hope, faith, and desire most of my life. All those qualities were challenged along the way. I held onto hope, so I would not die. I looked to strengthen my faith, so I could sustain hope.

Love was the most important ingredient to a successful life. What made me a whole person was learning to accept and love myself just as I was with all my shortcomings, fears, and handicap. This was the most valuable gift I gave to myself.

I am at an interesting time in my life. I find myself reflecting on my personal journey with a different set of eyes. I can see the value in all my experiences. I long to share what I have learned with as many people as possible. One thing that never escapes my mind is that at my birth, it was thought that I would not live. And here I am six decades later. We don't know what life has in store for us. It is a mystery that unfolds in due course. We have the power to choose how we will respond to life. That much, I know for sure.

Positive words heal. Negative words destroy. There is quite a difference between constructive criticism and negativity. Along the way, I learned that I do not have to own other people's negative viewpoints.

I am grateful that my mother did not accept the doctors' assessment at my birth. Her choice was wisdom in action. She did not know what disregarding the doctor would mean for me or my future, but something inside her told her to wrap me in a soft blanket and bring me home. That is an example of invisible courage.

We all have moments like that. Perhaps they are not so pronounced, like life and death situations. There are moments where something deep within us calls us to move through a situation in a certain way. There the mystery of life is revealed and the benefit of listening to our spirit is made visible. We make the beauty and purpose of what is invisible seen by our choices.

We cause love and compassion to be made visible by our good intent. This is what invisible courage means to me.

It is not the portion of my body that is missing that makes me who I am. My unique invisible courage was the goodness within me, longing to be shared.

The gifts I was born with were inside of me all along, waiting for me to allow it to rise like a seed through soil. The same is true for us all.

When I became employed in my forties, I was excited to work with people with disabilities. At first, the invisible courage I was bringing forward was simply being able to work and be paid for my work. That was an achievement and a goal I had set. What came next was the mutual gain between me and my consumers. In many instances, we elevated each other's life by our intentions. It was not long before I could see how those mutual relationships were developing into bridges capable of breaking down barriers. For decades, I had to break those barriers down by myself.

In my work, I was teaming together with people with disabilities, co-workers, and other community agencies to gain services for individuals. Together, we harnessed people's rights. I moved through the human service system during a time when people were acquiring more and more rights in the communities they lived in. Laws and building codes were being changed to make mainstream living accessible for people with varying disabilities. I was elevating awareness by using my voice on behalf of people who had lost theirs for whatever reason.

The work and the people taught me the value of inner strength and using our voice to make the world, or at least our part of the world, a better place.

Having matured in the life that was given to me, I learned that there are those who wish to destroy; there are people who knock down the bridges others work so hard to build. I could not support that in my life.

Even now, I am never completely removed from the hurt I experienced along the way. I can relate to injustice and, even worse, cruelty.

I get riled up talking about certain periods of my life and that is okay. I am passionate about my experiences. I want other people to understand their value, however they are. I believe that what many of us lack is faith and confidence in ourselves. We are defeated before we begin. This is one quality I wish to break down and replace with love and self-confidence.

I first had to believe I could do whatever I set my mind to

do. Then I had to figure out how I could achieve it. This is the gift of invisible courage. We take what is unseen and nurture it until it is seen. This is as old as time. My faith tells me God wishes us to knock down the negative view and build up the positive. That begins with us. We must make ourself right first, and then the rest follows.

Life has taught me so many things. People have shown me the way, even if their actions were misguided. They still show me sign posts for the direction I needed to go in.

Years ago, I was in my office working with one of my consumers. She felt as though nothing in her life was going right and she had a deep belief that nothing would. She came to me, defeated. It took a little while for her to understand that her own attitude was the block. She approached every opportunity as though it was already a failure. That was why nothing was working out for her. Once she could see that it was her point of view that needed attention, she gradually shifted her thinking from instant failure to possibility. Once she managed to redirect her thoughts, she began to live a life full of possibility. At that point, she got her life on track.

She found a job, a nice apartment, got her license, and created a better future for herself. Her invisible courage came forward and made all the difference in her life.

A friend of mine shared with me a great story. She was very depressed after having a few years of hardship and financial difficulties. For many years, she had been a professional caretaker and found herself taking care of her elderly mother, while raising two teenagers. She was exhausted and at a loss of what direction to move in. She felt trapped in a cycle of situations that never seemed to improve.

One Christmas Eve morning, she decided to do a good deed with the hope of shifting her energy. She put a bag of food together for a homeless man she had passed almost daily on her way to care for her mother. She decided this was the day she would acknowledge him and share some of what she had in her home, which wasn't much.

She drove to the street corner where the man held his sign, telling passersby that he was homeless. She pulled the car over and he calmly scurried to her window. She handed him the bag of food and asked how he was doing today. He looked down the highway and said, "There is no one out there who can help me." She replied, "There are people out there who can help you. You just have to let them." With that pearl of wisdom, they parted company smiling at one another.

She drove away, murmuring under her breath, "You got it right, buddy. There's no one out there who will help."

She later told me that whispering those words out loud was the best thing that ever happened to her. She had felt it deep inside. No one was helping her. What she had not realized was she wasn't letting anyone help her. Most people she knew were not even aware of her struggles. She hid the truth—even from herself. She raved for a long time that the homeless man on the street corner had changed her life. She could not get his words or hers out of her mind for months until she finally realized she had built a wall between her and anyone who cared about her.

That wall made it impossible for people to see what was really going on in her life and where they could help. It was not that they did not want to; they just did not know.

This moment in time for her took the invisible negative thinking and transformed it into invisible courage. Once she became aware of how she was blocking her growth, she made some changes. She got some help and some much needed rest. The world began to look brighter and she was beginning to feel at ease in her own life, less depressed and more able to be present to those who needed her.

She never forgot the words the homeless man had told her; that there was no one who would help. It became her mission to show people where they are building walls. Her invisible courage was taking the step to be honest enough with herself and realize where she needed to make changes.

After that, she was still a caretaker who had set some boundaries and let others help her.

Today, she is a productive person with a great deal of energy.

Brick-by-brick, we can build those walls, or we can build bridges. Both have completely different outcomes.

Dr. Wayne Dyer said, "The only limits you have are the limits you believe." When I received my driver's license, some-one said to me, "How can you drive? What if you get into an accident?" I replied by letting them know that my vehicle was designed so I could drive. I handle the van well and safely. I went on to say, "Why are you assuming the worse when this is a positive achievement for me?"

Right there, I exposed negative thinking. Invisible courage

is sort of like shining light where light may not enter. I believe we are all called to expose misconceptions.

With each next step I took to accomplish a goal or gain increased independence, I heard words of caution from people. I learned with each experience that, in most cases, individuals were trying to project their own fear about growing and taking risk onto me.

Once I was able to draw the line between constructive advice and the passing along of fear, my life became much more free.

I had plenty to take care of within my own thinking and life experience. I did not need to compound what I needed to work on for myself with the tangled thinking of another person.

The limits we find ourselves surrounded with are either placed there by others, or we place them there ourselves. Like an overflowing brook, we can find a way to allow our best self to flow out into the world and disregard negative influences.

We find our way, if we choose to carefully acknowledge what makes sense in our unique life and what does not.

I think back to the time I had the opportunity to speak before five hundred disabled children in São Miguel. My heart fills with joy even now, so many years later. I was willing to speak to the children and speak honestly. While I spoke, I was very impressed by the stillness in the room. It was amazing how attentive all the children were. These young souls needed to hear from someone who could relate to their experience. They wanted to hear my story and see me in action. The tone was so positive. They needed me to tell them how and why I learned to love myself. They also needed permission to love who they were, just as they were. In part, their silence was because they were studying me. Children are so inquisitive. They wanted to link my physical handicap with my personal story in a way that they could incorporate into their lives. They were intent on figuring out how I could have accomplished the things I had.

They were not castaways. They were not forgotten. I wanted them to know I saw them and loved them. "You are a valuable part of your family and society," I exclaimed.

There was one boy who touched my heart deeply. Reflecting on this experience that happened a decade ago, I realized I was learning about my invisible courage even then.

After the conference, he came to me and said, "Don't forget me. If you find a power wheelchair, don't forget me." The young boy, then about age 15, was telling me two things within his request. He wished for a power chair because he could understand that, based on my example, he could have command of his days if he had that level of independence. More importantly, he wanted to make sure I did not forget him. He wanted to be seen, heard, and valued. It took a lot of courage for him to speak up in that way. He was so grateful for our meeting that he gave me a necklace he'd made in school.

I never did forget him. The young man touched my heart deeply. He actually gave me courage to continue telling my story.

So much has changed since I was his age. The children were given a great deal more respect than I had been given as a young girl. They had support and they supported each other. My heart was filled with peace to see this. I was thrilled to witness the positive changes in the way people interacted with disabled people. I was pleased to be a part of that change in some small way.

To see the children so eager to hear my story and better their personal experiences instantly eased any lingering resentment I was harboring about my life experience. The example here was beautiful. At that conference, the children and I lifted each other to visualize our fullest potential.

That is what it is all about. We are called to lift each other up, not to knock anyone down.

Another lovely example of invisible courage in my life came when I was working with a disabled woman at my place of employment. She had a spinal issue that impaired the use of her arms and legs. She was a grown woman living with her aging parents. Having been cared for and sheltered, she had not acquired much in the way of independence. She came to me for help. I took a bold move to suggest she learn some independent living skills and then, together, we would find her an apartment. This was a radical step for her. It all made sense, though. Her parents would not live forever. At some point, she would be on her own. *Why not move in that direction at will rather than in frantic haste?*

This lady did not want any services or assistance. She had become used to relying on her parent to provide for her. This scenario was born out of love, but was counter productive.

I spent a great deal of time talking with her and sharing my experience. I let her know that by taking small steps toward independence, she would discover a whole new aspect of her life and purpose that she had not yet discovered. She began with getting herself a personal care attendant who could help her with washing herself, getting dressed, mobility, and more.

Allowing her mother to do these things kept her in the mindset of a little girl. Using the services of a personal care attendant who was a peer opened up channels for adult thinking and living.

After a period of time, we had worked on the small steps and she had gained more and more confidence in herself. She did realize she had much more ability than she'd thought. She was ready to move into her own apartment.

She was nervous but happy. This was one of the biggest steps she'd ever taken. Her parents were very happy for her. Her sister called me very happy for her sister. Her action toward independence gave everyone in her family a sense of joy and relief, knowing this woman was taking steps to take care of herself.

The family had a new apartment party for her. She received gifts items she would need for her new home. It was truly a celebration.

This lady began to thrive in her life. She had learned so much. She was dressing herself, preparing meals, and getting very creative finding ways to achieve her goals using her body as it was. For example, she would microwave a meal and use a spatula she held in her mouth. She would slip the spatula under the meal and balance it to the table. These things may not seem like grand accomplishments to a person who has use of their arms, but for a person who cannot, these little tricks mean a great deal. Every little success means so very much.

This delightful lady also had a pet cat. Now, instead of being taken care of, she was not only self-reliant, accepting assistance as needed, but she was also taking care of another living creature.

Her story then and now inspires me so much. Her invisible courage was shining.

The teacher and the student learn from one another. I have seen this over and over again in my life.

I wanted to share my story to help people who may not feel they have it within them to achieve their goals. I wanted to share my experience with all kinds of people, not only people with disabilities. We can all benefit from tapping into our courage that may be dormant for what ever reason. I learned new things about myself gathering my thoughts for *Invisible Courage*.

One thing was that I accepted myself even more deeply than I had prior. I wanted to be authentic in telling my story. Even now, there are times I become angry and frustrated. I allow myself to feel what I feel but I don't linger there. I do not wish to let emotions like anger and frustration rule my life. If someone looks away from me because of how I look, I try to let a smile set them at ease. If a clerk asks someone I am with, "What would she like?" I speak up for myself in that particular moment, gently raising awareness.

If I feel a sense of rejection, I quietly feel that emotion and feeling of being invisible.

Then I let it go. We are all doing the best we know how to do.

Those situations do bubble up old experiences. I tell myself, *I am not invisible and I do matter.* I make the deliberate choice not to resent the person who has offended me because I do not have to receive that action as an offense.

Most of the time, they are not being malicious. They are just uncomfortable and think they have to respond to me differently than they would another person who they perceive as no disability. Once again, it is a learning curve for us both. I hold the expectation that something good may come from the experience.

We have more ability within us than we know. Regardless of what our bodies look like, our beliefs, or any perceived differences, let us all find ways to tear down obstacles. Let us open channels of positive action and change. Let us all embrace our unique qualities and gifts. Let us all embrace our common ground. Most of all, let us all discover our glorious invisible courage.

*Melissa Robillard, Author of **Snowball's Great Adventure**
She inspired me to write my book.*

# On The Edge

by Janine Ouellette Sullivan

A poem of hope and of bringing our invisible courage forward.

*I was on the edge of something new*
*Something I could have only dreamed of*
*And I had*
*Never a word spoken to anyone*
*This was mine and mine alone*
*Privy only to God and my soul*
*Barely revealed to me until this moment*
*There on the water's edge*
*Tide rising*
*A symphony of rippling water*
*The Indian summer breeze*
*Leaves of poplar, birch, and elm*
*Sprinkle from the limbs*
*At the request of the southerly gust.*
*It was time!*
*Half-naked trees reaching to the heavens*
*I with them*
*Exposing my soul*

*Arriving*
*Never have I heard the song so clearly*
*Never has the emergence of bliss been so steady*
*I was on the edge*
*Edgy and bold So I did it. Finally.*
*Even the noon hour honored this time in silence*
*Beloved river you were as glass*
*She saw my eyes so clearly*
*Not a leaf moved*
*Nothing moved*
*Not bird or chipmunk.*
*Clouds stood still*
*As did time.*
*There, there it was all along*
*Daring to see its richness*
*Moving closer*
*And closer still*
*On the edge*
*Exposed so much so that fear itself ran away*
*Leaving me so suddenly, jolting me off balance.*
*Recovering, managing my stand*
*I was on the edge of something new*
*Something I could have only dreamed of*
*and I had.*

# Friend

A poem from my dear husband.

F    is for FILOMENA, a really true and good friend.

R    is for the RADIANT light that emits from her. It makes her a warm and caring person.

I    is for the IMMEASURABLE amount of faith that my friend has in the Lord, that seems to help her friends along.

E    is for the EDIFICATION that she shows for the Lord, who loves her very much and that she's in love with just as much.

N    is for the NATURAL friend that she is. There is nothing artificial about Filomena Diniz.

D    is for the DEDICATION to the Lord that my true friend, Filomena, has.

*Thank you for being my friend—FILOMENA!!!*
*God Bless You and Happy Birthday,*

Love, Jimmy
*October 8, 1994*

# Now Begin
# To Experience
# Your Invisible Courage!

# Workbook

At this point in *Invisible Courage,* perhaps you are curious enough about your own life to do some exploring. I have put together a series of questions that I feel are helpful for self-discovery. Nurturing yourself and your spirit should be a devotion that you take seriously. My hope is that these reflection exercises will prompt you to think of way to bring a fresh, new outlook to your life.

1.  Write about a time you felt people were unkind to you.

_____

_____

_____

_____

_____

_____

_____

_____

_____

2. Do you use negative language when talking about yourself?
   Why do you do this? When did it begin?

3. Write a word that diminishes your self-worth. Write why you use this word to describe yourself, or allow others to use this word when referring to you.

_____

_____

_____

_____

_____

_____

_____

_____

_____

_____

_____

_____

_____

_____

_____

_____

_____

_____

_____

4. Write about any actions you take in your daily life that hinder or block you from being happy or being the person you feel you could be.

_____

_____

_____

_____

_____

_____

_____

_____

_____

_____

_____

_____

_____

_____

_____

_____

_____

_____

_____

5. **List what makes you feel vulnerable.**

_____

_____

_____

_____

_____

_____

_____

_____

_____

_____

_____

_____

_____

_____

_____

_____

_____

_____

_____

Now, turn your thoughts in another direction.

6. **List three actions you can begin today that would improve your life.**

_____

_____

_____

_____

_____

_____

_____

_____

_____

_____

_____

_____

_____

_____

_____

_____

_____

_____

7. List ten positive words you can use to describe yourself. Write a detailed paragraph for three of the words and explain how the words represent you.

_____

_____

_____

_____

_____

_____

_____

_____

_____

_____

_____

_____

_____

_____

_____

_____

_____

8. Everything in life hinges on the condition of change. Change can be good. We cannot change others, but we can change ourselves and our attitudes. List three positive changes you can make in your daily life.

_____

_____

_____

_____

_____

_____

_____

_____

_____

_____

_____

_____

_____

_____

_____

_____

_____

9. What has been your greatest dream in life? Write a detailed description of this dream.

_____

_____

_____

_____

_____

_____

_____

_____

_____

_____

_____

_____

_____

_____

_____

_____

_____

_____

_____

_____

10. I end *Invisible Courage* with *Now Begin*. These are words I frequently use to motivate myself. Every new situation has a beginning. What new beginnings do you need so that you can thrive and grow? Write a detailed description about your desired new beginnings.

_____

_____

_____

_____

_____

_____

_____

_____

_____

_____

_____

_____

_____

_____

_____

_____

I am grateful that you have taken the time
to read *Invisible Courage.*

I would love to hear from you.

Contact me at filatprayer@comcast.net